RED
GALOSHES

The harrowing, relentless determination, ordinary and joyful stories of an abused wife, turned single mother who gained tractionon the rocky, slippery path to renewed hope and confidence.

ANN McCARTHY

Ann McCarthy (signature)

LifeRich
PUBLISHING

Ps. 37:3-24 (handwritten)

LifeRich Publishing is a registered trademark of The Reader's Digest Association, Inc.

LifeRich Publishing books may be ordered through booksellers or by contacting:

LifeRich Publishing
1663 Liberty Drive
Bloomington, IN 47403
www.liferichpublishing.com
844-686-9607

All scripture quoted unless otherwise indicated is from the New International Version (NIV).

Names and some details have been changed to protect identity and privacy of those involved.

ISBN: 978-1-4897-4755-6 (sc)
ISBN: 978-1-4897-4754-9 (hc)
ISBN: 978-1-4897-4806-5 (e)

Library of Congress Control Number: 2023911027

Print information available on the last page.

LifeRich Publishing rev. date: 06/09/2023

BOOK REVIEWS

Ruth Johnson
Legal Admin. Asst.
Devout Christian

"The stories [in this book] show life is messy, but God isn't afraid of the mess. *Red Galoshes* gives such a beautiful reflection of what our Father does for us through the messiest times of our lives: those we create and those that just happen because we live in a broken world. Each story helped me see God's relationship with us in such a beautiful light. I also loved the parenting ideas/tips and will be recommending my daughter read it when she has children."

Willow Mackenzie
Advocate for All

"Ann was able to display reality and hardships in a compassionate manner that makes her relatable. I like how she did not deny readers the horrid details, as it honestly portrayed the depth of the pain she went through and the hope and strength she gained in hard times. I appreciated how Ann included her own reactions, flaws, and errors. I also liked how her adventures with her children expressed love, adventure, and imperfection. Ann is an extremely brave and resilient woman who knows how to find joy in all things. Well done!"

George Shea, D. Min.
Served for twenty years as Professor of Pastoral Care for Women.
Author of two books on women's and emotional spiritual care.
Mother of two adult children and six grandchildren.

"Great story! Ann draws the reader in with her engaging narrative style, detailing with clarity the challenges of an abusive marriage. The reflections are extremely helpful to readers of many places of life. This book is a great resource and blessing to our world. This book is so needed! I STRONGLY BELIEVE THIS STORY IS ONE TO BE TOLD!"

Alexandria Peterson D. Min
Executive Director
Ministry Leader
Author of book on Marriage
Mother, Grandmother

"*Red Galoshes* displays a faith in God that is real and tangible. I loved Ann's stories of God's provision. Ann's ability to describe the setting and emotions keeps the reader engaged. This book becomes more interesting as you read, which was surprising for me, there was no plateau. *Red Galoshes* gives the reader hope for the future and draws them closer to God. Excellent book !"

D. G., MA (and my spiritual mentor)
Founder/Director of a Spiritual Development Ministry
Spiritual Director
Author of: a personal spiritual growth curriculum
and a spiritual memoirs book series
Mother of two, Grandmother of six

"*Red Galoshes* was as heart wrenching as it was uplifting. It is raw, up close and personal. It is encouraging to see how Ann depends on God and He comes through over and over again. *Red Galoshes* has a great message for those in similar circumstances. Even though I have not had the same personal experiences in my marriage, I decided Ann just might have something to say to me too. *Red Galoshes* is not dry, boring, or a downer. Though situations are not always good, Ann weaves hope throughout."

To My Children:

Because of you, I chose faith over fear and victory over being a victim.

Our experiences and your insights encouraged me to write my story.

CONTENTS

Acknowledgments xv

Foreword xvii

Preface xix

Editor's Note xxi

Introduction: I've Been There xxiii

Part 1 Childhood and Marriage 1

Only Thing Left 1

Red Galoshes 4

My Best Friend 6

The Ripple Effect 9

Part 2 Wife and Mother 13

Patterns of Behavior 13

It's a Trust Issue 16

Instability: Financial Abuse 19

Not a Submissive Wife: Spiritual Abuse 22

Intimacy: Sexual Abuse 26

The Goat 30

Protecting Him at My Cost 34

Sprinkling Salt...38

Emotional Abuse and Neglect 38

Psychological Abuse: Manipulation 39

Verbal Abuse...40

My Daughters..42

My Oldest: Marion..43

Second Oldest: Kay 44

Youngest: Cheri 45

My Sons 46

Oldest: William..47

Second Oldest: Thomas 48

Youngest: Ryan...48

My Children..50

Why Did I Stay?..51

The Bear 54

Part 3   Single Mom..57

New Beginning 57

A Step at a Time..60

Unclenched Hands 62

Stability: God Provides....................................65

Healing and Redemption.................................67

Mental Healing 67

Spiritual Healing 68

Divorce..68

Redemption...70

Edge of the World 71

Becoming Farsighted 74

Fearless Faith 76

Part 4　Single Mom with Teen/Adult Kids 80

　　Chicken Up 80

　　Memories Made Here 83

　　What Now? 86

　　Thomas's Story...90

　　Crying Is for Babies 94

　　Powerless 98

　　Our Ashes.. 101

Part 5　Advice and Reflection 104

　　Making the Most...104

　　Household Management..104

　　Friday Surprise..105

　　Family Meetings 105

　　Chores 106

　　Traditions 106

　　Thanksgiving and Preparing for Christmas..................... 107

　　Christmas 107

　　Christmas Party...108

　　Fun on a Budget 108

　　Parades 108

　　State Fair 109

　　Letting Kids Get Involved with Budget 109

　　Creative Mealtimes 110

　　Spontaneity...110

　　Single-Mom Friendship 111

　　Shared Reading Time 112

　　Conclusion 112

　　Teachable Moments.. 113

Conflict Calm Down... 113

Car Rides 114

Follow-Through and Expectations 115

Boundaries 115

Time Management 116

Discipline Roles and Types 116

Final Ideas 117

Reflections on Childhood... 118

Ryan... 118

Cheri 119

Thomas... 121

Wish I Had Known.. 122

Plan A: Conclusion 127

Bibliography... 131

ACKNOWLEDGMENTS

Amanda L. Greene, without you, this book would be a pile of stories reverberating in my mind, scratched out in journals, and hiding in the shadows. Thank you for helping me unpack these stories, allowing the light of truth and hope to filter in. As the trail master, you led these recollections along the path, forming a field guide with personal anecdotes as landmarks along the muddy, rocky road.

Freckles, you're pretty. There's a rainbow on your face.

L., you've got a friend.

Ladybug, I truly value your candid feedback and insight into the stories within these pages. You have been a constant encouragement, and I appreciate you so much. Your heart for others is an inspiration.

Pie, you have helped me see things in both a broader and sharper perspective in so many areas besides your feedback on this book. I am grateful for your support, critique, and sense of humor.

As iron sharpens iron, so one man sharpens another; further up and further in. What a time to be alive and following Jesus.

KitKat, you are the equalizer. You have a way of balancing and softening when approaching sensitive topics. Viewing even daily situations through an approachable lens. Your feedback has provided a viewpoint of leading with peace and love. All things great are wound up with all things little.

BeHe, I appreciate your open and gracious responsiveness to providing your perspective in honing sections of these stories. With all there is, why settle for just a piece of sky?

Barbara, your friendship is solid and true: faith-filled, time-tested, and resolute. Your encouragement is boundless, and your words are like apples of gold in settings of silver. I cherish our closeness and am grateful for your insight.

Beth, our friendship was raw, vulnerable, and faithful. While our paths have diverged, your friendship is a gem I treasure and admire.

Donna, my faith-filled colleague and friend, thank you for checking in on my writing and keeping me plugging along. You made me feel like what I had to share was worth setting my cap to and finishing. I've gained much from our numerous walks and talks.

Maxine, I feel our hearts knitted together as we long to reach struggling moms. You have been a genuine blessing. Thank you for speaking the reality of writing a book into existence.

FOREWORD

Not everyone can be described as courageous. But to actually meet someone who fits that description is extraordinary. My friend Ann McCarthy tells her story with confident transparency. As I read, my heart was amazed to see resilience through the eyes of a woman who endured an abusive marriage and raised six children, including one with a serious disability.

This book will take you on Ann's journey as God walked her through the hardest terrain of life. Ann does not take the shortcut around tough questions such as "Why did you stay so long? Why didn't you tell someone sooner?" With creativity and courage, she recalls the details of the abuse she experienced, exposing the unfortunate truth that abuse occurs even in Christian circles. Do not expect a plateau; this book holds your interest from story to story, from the beginning to the end. *Red Galoshes* also takes the reader to a panoramic view, showing not only Ann's perspective of the journey, but that of her children as well.

This spiritual memoir empowers readers with one word: "hope." Hope enabled Ann to do what they said could never be done: completing a masters' degree in speech pathology, (and now a doctorate!) successfully mentoring hundreds of single mothers and their children, becoming an active seminary speaker and community leader. This book inspires hope by reminding us that life is seldom if ever a straight path (Joseph's story in Genesis 37). Still, the God of the Bible is present and active, working in each moment of our journey to turn everything for our ultimate good.

Red Galoshes is the story of a woman who wouldn't give up, whose faith in Christ through heartache and disappointment ultimately leads to family triumph. It is the story of God's faithfulness, miracles, mercies, and love. This book leaves you with confidence that God is always there, weaving a beautiful mosaic out of the journey of our lives.

Maxine Lawrence

PREFACE

As I sit and write, my second cup of coffee has cooled. I drink it anyway. I have been contemplating the first part of Isaiah 40:31: "Yet those who wait on the Lord will renew their strength." To this day, people ask me how I did it. How did I have the strength to endure? Answer: On my knees. I kept in constant communication with God, a dialogue going throughout the day. Sometimes I waited on the Lord; sometimes I ran ahead. I learned as I went to lean on Him.

As a single mom of six kids, I needed divine intervention on a regular basis. Life often felt like pushing a boulder uphill, knowing that if I stopped, it would roll back on me. Hardly a day went by when I was not praying and waiting for God's strength, wisdom, and creativity.

Many single mothers I've encountered over the years have shared they feel encumbered and discouraged by responsibilities, stuck in familiar routines. My mind goes back to many Wednesday nights listening to single moms discuss why they couldn't do something: Why they couldn't go camping, why they couldn't go to the fair, why they couldn't go to the zoo, why they couldn't enjoy the rich experiences awaiting their families. The reasons included lack of finances, too hard to do without a man, and fear; because they had never gone on outings like this alone with kids. It saddened me to hear the restrictions they put on themselves and their families.

I was inspired by those moms to write this book. My hope is that if you are a single mom, my stories will ignite a spark of fearless faith and tenacity within you. Through my journey, I hope you will see Jesus can be your provision, protection, love, and creative inspiration, freeing you from shame, doubt, and fear.

For others, my hope is that my stories will help you better understand and empathize with the life of an abused wife and single mom in recovery from abuse. Let my stories inform your prayer life. Let them inspire you to help those who have been abused find the resources they need to heal and grow.

I also hope this book inspires everyone to create new memorable family moments with minimal resources, making the most of every day's opportunities. In the latter sections of this book, you will read the many ways God inspired me to make the everyday messes into memorable adventures.

It is important that you understand, this book is not a tell-all; it does not out anyone. I don't go into great length about the abuse I suffered. This book is not focused on the drama and tragedies, but on how through Christ I triumphed in difficult circumstances. The names of family and friends have been changed to protect their privacy. Although my friends, family, and children are a part of this story, this book's focus is my own personal and spiritual journey.

In Ephesians 6, we are instructed to suit up for a spiritual battle. Most days do not feel like a battle; just muddy and messy, slogging through daily routines, overdue bills, squabbling kids, and monotonous chores. Through these everyday experiences, we need to cinch up our waist with the belt of truth, wear the armored vest of righteousness, put on the shoes of the gospel of peace, hold high our shield of faith, and secure our helmet of salvation. By doing so, we strap on our red galoshes of joy and dare the messy, muddy events of everyday life to try and dampen our spirits.

You are about to join me on a rocky road. You will experience daring, suspense, sadness, pain, discovery, joy, and laughter. So grab your spoon, get comfy, and let's dig in.

EDITOR'S NOTE

There is much we can learn from the journeys of those who have been there, those with the courage to share their hardships and triumphs along the way. Listening to these stories helps us be seen, heard, and fill us with hope.

In *Red Galoshes*, Ann McCarthy invites us into her life's stories. Ann's spiritual memoir focuses on her personal perspective on experiences in her spiritual journey, moments where her relationship with God had a significant impact on her decisions.

Each part of this memoir is a collection of stories from a specific season of Ann's life. Each chapter includes an experience followed by a reflection. These reflections contain Ann's thoughts in hindsight as well as encouragement that connects Ann's journey to our own.

So put on your Red Galoshes and trek, stomp, and dance through the mire and beauty of Ann's hardships and triumphs. Let her stories encourage and empower you. Once you are done, take those galoshes with you, to guide you on your journey ahead.

Amanda L. Greene

INTRODUCTION

I've Been There

I guess now is a good time to give you a snapshot of my journey. To all the phrases below, know "I've been there." Maybe as you read these phrases, you will think about your own journey and find yourself saying, "Hey, I've been there too."

Military brat: My dad retired after a career in the Air Force, which meant we moved a lot and had many international and Stateside adventures.

Left college to get married: I was one year away from graduating with my bachelor's degree.

Stay-at-home mom: For ten years, I enjoyed being available for my kids, being in their lives, taking part in exploring and expanding their interests, being a homemaker, and planning activities for our family.

Raised a big family: I gave birth to six remarkable children, three girls and then three boys, all a year and a half (or less) apart.

Had a medically fragile child: Will, my fourth child and first son, was born with severe cerebral palsy; he used a wheelchair, was fed through a G-tube fed, was nonverbal, and was a blessing to our family.

Been in an abusive relationship: The man I married had a volatile temper, which did not present until my first child was eight months old. My husband became increasingly controlling, abusive, and unfaithful as the years went on.

Became a working mom: I secured a full-time position and worked in a local school district for six years before going back to college to earn my degree.

Went back to school full time, while working full time: Six months after my oldest graduated from high school, I graduated with my bachelor's degree. Six months after she graduated from college, I graduated with my master's degree.

Single mom: Raising my kids, I was always stretched in several directions at once. Being the only parent means being the go-to for all things, actively involved in homework, sports, music, clubs, church, and so on.

Had a child die: It was an unspeakable shock, pain, and grief. The loss and despair are deeper than any words can express.

Had a child come out as gay: Hearing this news caused tears, shock, and grief. We cried together and now are learning to maintain an open relationship.

Reflection

All of these "I've been there" statements are stories in their own right. This is the tip of the iceberg. However, I do want to make one thing clear: There is no way on this earth I could have come out of what I did, done the things I've done, built friendships I have along the way, loved my children, picked myself up from despair, and so much more without being on my knees. The most important thing to know is that my life is grounded in my relationship with the Lord Jesus Christ: He is unshakable.

It is my hope that you are able to relate to my experiences and are encouraged to share your stories. Through each of these experiences, I was not alone. Know that you too are not alone. As we open up to one another, darkness, loneliness, and fear dissipate. When we share our stories, we find common ground and can begin to empathize, strengthen one another, and spur each other on. Need a good book with stories you can connect with and be uplifted by? I've been there. And if you've been there or want to understand someone who has, then this book is for you.

PART 1

Childhood and Marriage

❖

Only Thing Left

It all began the day I was born. (I love starting like that because it is humorous and true.) My dad was stationed at Clark Air Force Base, near Manila in the Philippines. In June 1964, the most destructive typhoon since 1882 hit Luzon Island. A shocking 275,000 people were left homeless, and many died. The largest warship in the Philippine Navy sank as a result of Winnie's strong winds, registering past 118 miles per hour.

Two days after I was born, the typhoon hit Manila. Soon thereafter, I contracted salmonella from contaminated water in my bottle. I became so dehydrated that nurses had to cut into my skin to access my veins to draw blood and place IVs.

In addition to this, I had what was called intussusception of the bowel; my intestine had telescoped inside itself. I had abdominal surgery to repair the intussusception but cried so hard, I split the stitches open, twice. They ended up sewing my abdomen with copper wires. After all this, I was dying. The doctors told my parents they had done all they could.

So the Air Force flew my entire family to the United States, hoping a teaching hospital in Gainesville, Florida, could save my life. A doctor came to my parents and said, "We have done all we can do to save her. The only thing left to do is pray."

When my dad was nine, he became a Christian. Although my mom went to church, she had not chosen a relationship with Jesus Christ. But there was a chapel in that hospital, and my parents went there and prayed to save my life.

Right after they finished praying, there was a call over the PA system, asking them to come to my room; the doctors exclaimed that something had changed. My immune system had kicked in; I was showing overall improvement.

It was the answer to their prayers, and my mom gave her life to Jesus. I remained in the hospital for three months before my family could bring me home.

Reflection

As I think back on those doctor's words, I wonder, *Why is it we often think of prayer as the only thing left?* In the mindset of the medical world, prayer is a last resort. So often, we strive to force pieces of our life's puzzle together. It is not until the pieces do not fit that we turn to prayer. There is no shame in wanting to help, to feel like we are doing our part. We crave a chance to physically respond to show we care and to solve problems. But our efforts may be in vain if we move ahead on our own.

Psalm 139:1–18 has been a source of comfort and peace for me since I was a teen. It says,

> Lord, you know me. For you created my inmost being; you knit me together in my mother's womb.

I praise you because I am fearfully and wonderfully made … your eyes saw my unformed body; all the days ordained for me were written in your book before one of them came to be.

This scripture reminds us of God's sovereignty in all situations, across the span of space and time. We can feel comfort and peace because of His constant presence, power, and knowledge. This chapter in the book of Psalms brings me rest when I am facing the unknown. There is no situation that sets the Lord back on His heels. Nothing causes Him to gasp in shock of the unexpected. There is no place too dark or anguish too deep that He cannot meet us there. He is sovereign, and we can trust His plan, even if we don't understand His reasoning. He is unshakable, compassionate, good, and powerful. It is because of these truths that we should include Him in each endeavor before we dive in.

So I encourage you to pray continuously; make constant communication with God a habit. This will keep you from not only making prayer a last resort but also keeping Him at the forefront of your mind. When we learn to seek Him first, we find rest in His care, gain wisdom from His counsel, and draw on His strength when we are weak. When we experience His rest, wisdom, and strength, we are better able to face uncertain terrain without fear. This way, when troubled times come and you are in survival mode, you will be less tempted to try to tackle things on your own but to seek Him first.

When I was young, my dad and I would spend evenings listening to his music on records. One worship song that resonates so deeply with me is "You Are My All in All." Its lyrics say

> You are my strength when I am weak
> You are the treasure that I seek
> You are my all in all
> When I fall down you pick me up

When I am dry You fill my cup
You are my all in all.

We all need to include God in our daily moments so He is our all in all. This way, praying is not the last thing but the first thing we think to do. Just like the first thing we do before leaving the house is to put on a pair of shoes.

Red Galoshes

In 2014, I took a job as a speech-language pathologist with a very long commute. Every two weeks, I flew from Portland, Oregon, to Bethel, Alaska. On the weekdays, I village-hopped in a small propeller plane to elementary schools along the Bering Sea. If a flight was canceled due to poor weather conditions, I worked in the Bethel area.

In April, the temperature in Bethel rose a bit above freezing, warming up to 36 degrees. Months of frozen snow and ice began to melt. Mounds of dirty, gray snow bordered the roadsides. As I picked my way through puddles while walking to the elementary school, I thought back on my long-forgotten red galoshes.

When I was six, we lived with my grandma in Grand Rapids, Michigan, while my dad prepared a home for us at his military post in Germany.

I remember I didn't like the beginning of spring. This was when the snow melted and turned into a slushy, muddy mess. The mounds of dirty, gray sludge got pushed to the sides of the roads.

As I got ready each day, I put my outer gear on at the door: mittens, hat, coat, and my bright-red galoshes.

What I loved about my galoshes was the way dirty puddle water splashed up against them and slid right off. Those red galoshes covered and protected my feet as I walked to school, navigating the mush of melted snow puddles and dirty snowbanks.

Try as it may, the slush and mud could not penetrate those rubber shields. In fun, I would mock the puddles, knowing they could not dampen my shoes, my socks, or my spirits.

Reflection

As I think back on those mucky days, I realize that life often feels like the beginning of melting spring: muddy and messy. We feel this in our daily struggles: a flat tire, a sick child, an unrelenting boss, not enough time to accomplish our to-do list, and so on. The demands pile up like dirty snow we have to trudge through.

When raising my six children, I remember these messy moments when a kid was sick but I was needed at work and felt pulled in two directions. Or the time my daughter had car trouble at the same time her brother had a concert at the high school. No matter what I chose, I left someone else stuck in the muck, and I was left trudging through the strain of letting someone down. Wishing I could be in two places at once, I felt inadequate. Over the years, I marched on through many sludge-filled messes like these.

As you will soon read, I have experienced abuse, financial instability, and a child with special medical needs, to name only a few. But like those bright-red galoshes, God has been with me protecting, covering, and shielding me with His armor. God's armor is not just for the wars of life. He has equipped us also for the everyday battles, the muddled parts of life. We know we do not fight against humankind but need this equipment for the spiritual battles and struggles of life. (For more details on the armor of God, see Ephesians 6:13–17.)

No matter what mess life brings, if we allow Him to be, God is there. His armor protects us. It is with this truth that I have been able to move forward with confidence: full of joy and hope. In the mucky, difficult, and dirty moments of our everyday lives, this is where we need to strap on our red galoshes. With God's presence, we know circumstances cannot dampen our shoes, socks, or spirits. For me, learning to build a personal relationship with God in childhood was a necessary foundation for the years to come.

My Best Friend

When I was six years old, we moved to Germany, where my family attended the chapel on base. One Sunday evening there, unprompted, I gave my heart to Jesus. As young as I was, I understood the commitment I was making. To this day, I clearly remember the light-as-air feeling of joy as I walked back to rejoin my elated and proud family.

During our years in Germany, my relationship with the Lord grew. We had a hill in front of our apartment that overlooked a farmer's field and the woods. I would sit on that hill many times during the week, talking and listening to Him, sometimes for hours. I was told that talking to Jesus was like talking to a friend who is always there. I took that to heart, a fact as concrete as the concept of gravity. I did not question whether or not He was listening or would respond; because that's what friends do; sometimes, friends just listen and nod.

One of my dad's favorite hymns was "What a Friend We Have in Jesus." The first part of that hymn is:

> What a Friend we have in Jesus,
> All our sins and griefs to bear!
> What a privilege to carry
> Everything to God in prayer!
> O what peace we often forfeit,
> O what needless pain we bear,
> All because we do not carry
> Everything to God in prayer!

As a child, it seemed ridiculous not to bring everything to Jesus, my friend, as this song expresses. I learned to rely and depend on Him to protect me; I learned to lean on and trust in Him.

In this season, I looked up to my older brother Rick, who encouraged me to read a chapter of the Bible every day. So in the second grade, I would hold a Bible study at recess for any student who wanted to sit with me. It's kind of funny, because in second grade, I don't even know what my reading level was. But I knew the Bible was God's Word, and He wanted me to share it.

When I was eleven, my dad was transferred back to the States. He retired from the Air Force soon after, and we moved to Winter Park, Florida, to be near my grandmother.

My grandmother and I became very close. She was a godly woman and encouraged me to seek God for guidance to navigate life's journey. Throughout the early years of my faith, God confirmed His truth to me through scripture, songs, sermons, and speaking words directly to my mind and heart. Whenever I had a lot on my mind, I would retreat to my grandmother's spare bedroom. I called it my thinking place. I would bring my Bible and my journal, and stay for a weekend, sorting out the gray and messier parts of life with God.

Reflection

Looking back, as a young girl and a new believer, it was intuitive that God was close to me. The faith of my child's heart believed without doubt that He is who He says He is and He does what He says He will do. I am thankful for that firm foundation I could return to as an adult when I strayed from that close relationship.

Jesus speaks to our relationship with Him in John 15:5, where it says, "I am the vine; you are the branches. If you remain in me and I in you, you will bear much fruit; apart from me you can do nothing."

As the branches depend on the vine for life, we depend on Jesus.

To abide in Him is to train our mind and heart to focus on His presence. Meditation sometimes sounds like sitting cross legged on a pillow and tuning out the world. And while our quiet time with God should include tuning out distractions, it is not *that* type of meditation. It is more about being open to Him, aware of how He is working. On life's journey, if we let Him, He can be our guide and compass.

Some may ask, why bother to pray, if He already knows what we are thinking and what we are going to say? Well, why confide in your close friend when she already knows your faults, or when she's heard your stories a hundred times before?

We do it to share life together. God wants to share life with us, to have an ongoing conversation with us.

Nothing has helped me understand God more than being a parent. Our children may ask us for the reason why; however, we don't always answer their requests in the way they would like us to. This is usually because we know the plans we have for them, for our family, for their time, and so on. They don't need to know the details. They just need to know we've got this handled, and they can trust we have their best in mind.

We need to adopt that same attitude with God as His children. When it feels like our requests or questions are unanswered, we need to remember He has His best in mind for us.

I lost sight of this foundational belief at certain points in my life. But this truth was an underpinning to which I would return. Psalm 71:17 feels like it speaks directly to me: "Since my youth, God, you have taught me, and to this day I declare your marvelous deeds."

It was this Teacher I ran back to when my life changed dramatically as a mother of six. It is that friend, my Best Friend, I sought. Just as I practiced in my grandma's home, I would spend hours pouring my heart out to Him, listening, waiting expectantly, watching. I found stability and courage, regaining my footing on solid ground. like my red galoshes,

I encourage you to take the time to get closer to Jesus, to invest in an ongoing, reciprocal conversation with God throughout the day. Abide in Him, rest in Him, listen to Him. Begin reading the Bible; meditate on the truths found in His words. Become acquainted with His ways, and by doing so, you will build a relationship with your Best Friend.

The Ripple Effect

My childhood friendship with my Best Friend changed as I grew into adulthood. After my first year at Valencia Community College in Orlando, I was ready to get away from the humidity and bugs of Florida. So I went to live with my brother and his family in Portland, Oregon, with the hope of attending Multnomah Bible College.

Not long after, my parents and grandma moved to Portland as well. Then at the very young age of forty-eight, my dad was diagnosed with Alzheimer's disease. My brother, mom, dad, and I went to meet with pastors and professors at Multnomah, who anointed my dad with oil and prayed over him. I begged God for healing. I believed with all my heart He would, yet my father continued to deteriorate.

Meanwhile, in my second year at Multnomah, I had an assignment to interview ten random people about their worldview and spiritual beliefs. I had procrastinated and, with the due date looming, used my workplace: a car dealership, to get the assignment done. I made up surveys and passed them out on clipboards to salesmen.

One of the salesmen followed up on the survey. He was raised by a mom who was a devout Jehovah's Witness and a dad who did not practice any spiritual belief. He had questions for me about Christianity and the Bible, so we decided to meet for a while over coffee or a meal.

When we started meeting, his spiritual condition was foremost in my mind. However, it quickly turned into what is referred to in Christian communities as "missionary dating." Then one day, he claimed to have made a decision to follow Christ, and I believed him, because I wanted to. He presented himself as financially stable and good with money. In my worries about the future, it felt like he could take good care of my mom when my dad no longer could. I put my faith in my perception of stability rather than in God.

I was acting out of line with what the Word of God states. We had become sexually active, which also skewed my reasoning. This warped and broke my relationship with God, interrupting clear communication. Not long after, we had a false pregnancy alarm. When that happened, I resigned myself to the fact that I would spend the rest of my life with this man and decided to make the best of it. I tried to paint a rosy picture in my mind of what a happy family we could be.

So when he proposed, I was ready and said yes. I quit school in June of my second year because I was going to be a wife now (I know, ancient thinking). My parents believed what I said, that he was a Christian. I wasn't lying to them but knew inside this wasn't *all* right. If nothing else, I was farther along in my spiritual life and faith walk than he was. I would have turned on a dime if my parents had said they did not agree with me being engaged. I was waiting for that; it was my litmus test. But my parents were supportive. They did not express concern.

My brother, on the other hand, did not feel this was right or good. His objections stirred up family discord. I got a call from a fellow church youth ministry leader the morning of my wedding, asking me not to go through with it. It was too late. This time, I was pregnant. We were married that October.

Reflection

Thinking back on this time, I realize I hid in the shame of being sexually active before marriage. That shame made my life mucky and slippery; it skewed my ability to listen to wise counsel and even affected my self-esteem. I had to marry this man now. I could not listen to anyone's counsel because they were counseling me on what they did not know. Proverbs 11:14 says, "Where there is no guidance, a people fall" (ESV).

Sadly, I am not the only one who paid the price for my choices. My husband, my children, my brother, his family: We all bear scars from foolish decisions I made in my shame.

I see the consequences of my actions fell on them. In Exodus 20:5–6, Exodus 34:6–7, and Numbers 14:18, the Bible speaks to the consequences of the father visiting the children and grandchildren. Descendants from generation to generation may struggle with similar issues due to what was modeled in parental behavior. Children pick up on more than we realize. A parent or grandparent may not be aware of how their thoughts, words, and behaviors are affecting others.

As I raised my kids, I taught them about how our choices affect everyone around us. I reminded them of how when a rock is thrown into a lake, it creates a ripple effect on the water, circles continually moving out from that initial kerplunk. I explained the same was true with our actions, words, and choices; they affect our circle of influence.

As long as we continue to act on lies about our identity, circumstances, or who God is, we are stuck slipping and sliding on gray icy snow. But the good news is, Proverbs 11:14 also says, "but in an abundance of counselors there is safety" (ESV) And in James 5:16, we are told, "Therefore confess your sins to each other and pray for each other so that you may be healed. The prayer of a righteous person is powerful and effective."

We are encouraged to own up to one another about incidents where we've done wrong or had wrong motives. We are not told to do this because it increases our shame but to release us from the burden. When we can say to a trusted friend, brother, or sister, I am struggling with this, or I am ashamed of that, together in support and prayer, it brings us to deliverance, helping us find a path to safety, allowing us to find solid ground with God.

When my kids had a blow-up, I would often have them not only apologize to the one they offended, but also to the whole family. By doing this, I taught them that when you act out, it makes a mess everyone has to clean up. This meant that I too apologized when I blew up.

It is hard to think past the moment. It is hard to realize the decisions you make today will affect others tomorrow. But Psalm 139 encourages us and tells us He knows and understands us; He is never far from us. God is all powerful, and that power is at work within us. Ephesians 3:20 says, "Now to Him who is able to do immeasurably more than all we could ask or imagine, according to His power that is at work within us." If we confess our poor choices, we can find grace, freedom, and support for ourselves and generations to come. This breaks us free from the cycle of shame and the patterns of behavior that keep us and those we love stuck in the muck.

PART 2

Wife and Mother

Patterns of Behavior

Years later, when I was leading a single moms group, I invited the founder of Abuse Recovery Ministry Services (ARMS) to speak to a small group at my church. As I listened, I was surprised as old wounds reopened and frightful memories came back. My husband and I went through every abuse cycle she described, every behavioral pattern, again and again.

The presenter explained the first phase: "Tension Building." During this period, the abuser feels ignored, threatened, annoyed, or wronged. The feeling can last as short as several minutes, but as long as several months.

My mind went back to when my first born was eight months old. We had recently moved because my husband became finance manager of a car dealership. One morning, my daughter cried from her crib in our room upstairs. My husband went up to take care of her, but she kept crying for me. I went upstairs and saw her gasping

13

for breath between cries. She saw me and with pleading eyes reached her little arms reached out to me. My husband held her tight and said no, *he* was taking care of her. My heart longed for her; sometimes, a child just needs her mom.

The guest speaker then described the second phase: "Incident." This phase may begin with verbal abuse or psychological abuse (or both). Then abusers attempt to gain control or dominate through violence. They often excuse their behavior by blaming, accusing, or faulting the victim. I reached for my daughter to reassure her. My husband, who was seated on the bed, reared back and kicked me in the stomach, hard, sending me backwards. I was hurt and shocked because I was pregnant with our second child. Stunned and dismayed, I went downstairs. After a few minutes, he came to the railing overlooking the main floor and threw a glass bottle down, ordering me to make her a bottle. The glass shattered all over the kitchen floor. Shortly after this, he left for work. My mind raced, I had never experienced anything like this in my life! I consoled and comforted my daughter but went through the day stunned.

The speaker said these incidents are followed by a time of "Reconciliation or Honeymoon." In this phase, the perpetrator may feel remorse, guilt, or fear that their partner will leave or call the police. The abuser gives assurances it will never happen again, or they will do their best to change. They will show affection and apologize or alternatively ignore the incident. The abuser may even use self-harm or threats of suicide to gain sympathy or prevent the relationship from ending. Abusers are often convincing, and victims are often eager for the relationship to improve. The victims feel pain, fear, humiliation, disrespect, and confusion and may mistakenly feel responsible. Abusers are often convincing, and victims are often eager for the relationship to improve. So many times, the survivors (who are worn down and confused by long-standing abuse) stay in the relationship.

I spent the day going through the motions, numb. My thoughts were whirling. I wanted to call my mom and talk to her but was afraid to share what had happened that morning. After work, my husband came home, very apologetic. He brought flowers and dinner. He vowed it would never happen again and declared his undying love for me. I was willing to forgive and start over. I wanted to put it behind us and move on. I did not realize this was the beginning of a pattern that would replay over the next several years.

The last phase she described was "Calm." During this phase, the relationship is relatively calm and peaceable. The abuser may agree to counseling and create a normal atmosphere. Over time, the abuser's apologies and requests for forgiveness become less sincere and are stated mostly to prevent separation or intervention. Interpersonal conflict inevitably arises, leading again to the tension-building phase and starting the cycle all over again.

We lived in that home for close to a year before he quit his job, and we moved to a different city, where he took a new job. No other abuse happened in that home or the next; a period of calm. However, I found out years later, during this calm, he was having an affair. I suspected it at the time but had no way to prove it.

Reflection

I had never experienced abuse growing up. I felt alone and was unaware of any resources or teaching on abuse. Having an awareness of the sickness eating away at my family could have changed my experiences.

Also, I didn't tell anyone about what I was going through. I figured it was my marriage, my relationship, my problem to deal with. If I had known, I may not have been so quick to let it go, move on, and start fresh each time. I may have sought counseling and been less tolerant of his excuses and apologies.

With this in mind, I would encourage you to pray and be willing to ask yourself the tough questions: Have I seen this pattern of behavior in my marriage or family? Can I share a story of my own like this one, labeling the phases? Do I have friends or family who have shared their story with me? Have I observed this pattern while with my friends or family?

Here is some information that may help provide perspective: In the United State, one in four women experience physical abuse from their intimate partner, and one in seven men will. Emotional abuse is found in 80 percent of marriage relationships. On average, 40 percent of men and women report aggression or forceful/violent control in their relationship. Assess your relationships. If you believe you are experiencing abuse, there are resources available; you are not alone. Please see the resources section of this book for help.

I am hopeful this information will help those in domestic violence situations reach out, seek help, and change their circumstances. For those not suffering, I would ask you to please be aware, be sensitive, and don't judge.

The following chapters share more stories and examples of how hard life can be in an abusive relationship. Although these stories are my personal experiences, the statistics show I am not alone. I encourage you to read my life stories with these questions in mind and learn from my personal journey.

It's a Trust Issue

After my husband and I had been married five years, I felt a great sense of desperation. He was barely working. We had three girls and our son William to provide for. Our budget was so tight we didn't have money for basic needs. Still, my husband was very controlling with our money. Because I brought no income into the household, he made me ask for money and accounted for every single penny. It was demeaning.

It started by accident. My daughter put a store item in the back of the stroller while we were at the mall. I didn't realize it until we were loading into our Suburban in the parking lot. I had all the kids with me, and it was a small item. I was not going to unload all of the kids, the stroller, and the wheelchair for William, then march back into the mall to return it.

After this incident, it dawned on me: I could hide unpurchased items in the diaper bag or stroller. There were times when we needed diapers or other smaller items we couldn't afford, so I took what we needed.

It was my youngest daughter's birthday, and I wanted to make her a cake. So I slipped a cake mix and frosting into the diaper bag. I had some necessities in the cart: milk, bread, laundry soap, and eggs. I went through the line, paid for the items, and began walking out of the store. But I was called back in by security.

William and one of my girls went with me upstairs to an office. An officer was present as well as the store managers. They asked me to remove the contents of the diaper bag. I was mortified. I explained that my daughter's birthday was coming up, and we couldn't afford the extra items for a birthday cake. Shaking, I apologized over and over again.

A woman manager said with disdain, "There are food stamps you could apply for to help you out." They let me go with a warning and took all of the stuff for the birthday cake.

I was so ashamed. I had been trying to solve my husband's financial problems on my own. I believed I could close the financial gap with illegal activity. I told myself I would pay the stores back. The truth was, our circumstances were gray, messy, and I had little control over them. I could not force my husband to work more. Plus, I could not get a job with little ones to raise and with Will's special needs.

As I sat there in the parking lot, I made a vow to God that I would never steal again. I would look to God to protect us and provide for our needs, no matter the season we were in.

I have never stolen again. If the temptation ever arose, I was reminded of my vow to trust Him.

Six years later, I was working to make ends meet off of one small paycheck and government support. Our refrigerator and cupboards were bare; we had a way to go before another paycheck.

One day, on our way home from church, my kids asked me, "Mom, what are we going to do?"

I said, "We are going to pray." When we got home, we got on our knees in a circle in the living room and prayed for God to take care of our needs.

That night, my community group from church showed up with more food than we had room for in our refrigerator, freezer, and cupboards combined. They even bought us a deep freezer (which I still have) and several gallons of milk: all the staples a home needs. Through others, the Lord provided above and beyond what I hoped.

Reflection

When I stopped trying to trudge through the financial sludge on my own, God blessed us, and our faith grew. Philippians 4:6 says, "Do not be anxious about anything, but in every situation, by prayer and petition, with thanksgiving, present your requests to God." My kids saw evidence that God listens; He answers prayers.

God never promises everything will be smooth sailing; in fact, in John 16:33, Jesus says we will have trouble. Raising my kids often felt like a gray, mucky trail with insurmountable barriers. Yet it is reassuring to know He isn't oblivious or uncaring. He understands our struggles. Hebrews 4:15 says, "For we do not have a high priest who is unable to sympathize with our weaknesses, but one who in every respect has been tempted as we are, yet without sin."

When I was in survival mode, I had forgotten that God will take care of our needs. Philippians 4:19 reminded me, "my God will supply every need … according to his riches in glory in Christ Jesus."

I encourage you to put your trust in God. Be real with your kids. Pray with them, bringing your concerns together before the Lord. Then you can rejoice when you see answers to prayer and your children's faith will grow. This way, your children will learn to turn to God as their provider.

Instability: Financial Abuse

For a season, my son and his wife lived with me while they saved money to buy their own home. One evening, they sat on the couch in the living room with their bills. As they began going over their finances, I was cringing. I braced myself for an unpleasant outcome, for the accusations and anger.

Instead, I was surprised; they were laughing and joking. There were no demands or reprimands. I truly was amazed and relieved.

A day or so later, I complimented them. I said it was a blessing to see a healthy way for a husband and wife to manage money together.

In my own marriage, the budget and finances were handled very differently. When my husband and I were engaged, he left a job without warning and without another job securely in place. He was irate when he told me he quit because another manager was being a jerk. (He used other words.) I sympathized with him and supported his decision, telling him there were other jobs.

Once we got married, I had six months until my student loans needed repayment. He refused to make payments, saying his name was not on the loan agreement. I was not working and had no control over the finances, so my loans went into default.

In the first two years we were married, we moved four times because he would quit a job every time his nose got out of joint. During this instability, he was moody, sullen, and angry; he blamed me for small issues. One time, he was late to his job. He decided to tell them he was late because the tires on his car got slashed. He hung up the phone, went out to his car with a knife, and slashed two of his tires! I could not believe what I had witnessed!

Then he finally landed a solid job. We were doing well financially, so our marriage seemed good. He enjoyed being generous. He held this job for three years, until they hired a woman manager, and then he quit without warning. Verbally, I was empathetic and supportive, but inside, I was disappointed and concerned. He got a similar job with a different company soon after, but it paid considerably less. It was like he was on a mission to self-sabotage but was taking all of us on this roller-coaster ride with him.

He would say the money he brought in was his and often brought up, with resentment, that I wasn't contributing financially. Yet he did not want me to work, so he could hold it over me that he was the breadwinner.

During the course of six years, he was given $40,000 two different times. One was inheritance from his mother's estate, the other a settlement from a car accident. Both times, I suggested money be set aside, put into a high-interest savings account, so we could use it for a down payment on a home. I cannot say what became of his inheritance - I just don't know, but he took the accident settlement and went on a spending spree.

In addition to these experiences, he did not file taxes. I told him I was afraid he would end up in jail and asked him to file year after year. My requests were met with apathy or laughter. I could not file the taxes because none of the income was in my name, and I did not have access to his W-2 forms.

Reflection

When your spouse controls the money, withholds financial information from you, keeps you from working (or forces you to work), takes your money, makes you ask for money, or refuses to give you money, these are forms of financial abuse.

My husband and I would regularly sit at our dining room table while he balanced the checkbook. I had to account for each penny spent. I understand that "giving each dollar a name" is a smart way to find out where your money is going, but these were not pleasant times. I was under scrutiny, and we were not equals. I was being treated like a child. I hated it; I was uncomfortable and scared because I didn't have all of the answers.

1 Timothy 5:8 says, "Anyone who does not provide for their relatives, and especially for their own household, has denied the faith and is worse than an unbeliever." I bore the burden of a household struggling financially, yet I was powerless. I was partnered with a man who I had to ask to take care of our family's needs. This verse came to mind several times over the years as he left significant repairs unattended. I thought of it when he squandered money on self-centered pleasures while bills were left unpaid. I never mentioned this scripture, as it would have led to either no response or an angry, violent outburst. I kept this biblical truth between the Lord and me, knowing that God saw, and I knew I could trust Him.

It is true that no one wants to share about their struggles. When we are embarrassed, we don't want people to know we are having trouble making it. However, God never wants us to live in shame or fear. He allows us to experience shame as a way to bring us to Him, to ask for forgiveness, to ask Him to take burdens off our minds and hearts.

When our children do something wrong, we want them to feel ashamed, but only temporarily. We use those feelings as an opportunity to help our kids understand who they've hurt and their perspective. It is the opportunity to help them admit to their wrong choice, ask for forgiveness, and move forward.

If you are experiencing financial abuse, do not let this behavior be a marital or family secret. Talk about it with a close friend, relative, counselor, or church leader. This way, you are no longer alone; there is someone you can turn to who knows the background.

After this, start putting money aside, bit by bit. You can secure it with that trusted friend or relative. This will help you not live in fear or at the controlling whim of the abuser. Doing this may make you feel fearful and deceitful. Pray about it. Ask God's blessing for provision and protection.

Consider the good wife spoken of in Proverbs 31. She is strong, dignified, and resourceful. She purchases a field and runs a business. She takes care of her family's needs while being wise and kind. This woman walks with the Lord and is respected and admired by her husband and her children. Notice, this woman does not live in fear or shame. Her husband is not intimidated by her and does not attempt to control her. This is a loving and respectful relationship with a healthy financial balance.

My final suggestion here is to seek counseling. If your spouse refuses to go, go by yourself. This will help you reason with a clear mind. You will be encouraged and strengthened to do the right thing for yourself and your family.

What causes you to hang your head, to drag your feet in the mud of life? Talk it over with God and give these issues to Him. He will lighten your step; He will encourage you and support you. He will help you stomp through the puddles of lies that have left your head hanging. Psalm 3:3 says, "But you, LORD, are a shield around me, my glory, the ONE who lifts my head high." God will guide you with your next steps and lift you up.

Not a Submissive Wife: Spiritual Abuse

One summer, when the kids were ages three to eight, we went on a camping trip with my brother's family in Sisters, Oregon. We packed bags for three nights over the Fourth of July weekend. We were looking forward to the hot dry days, cold starry nights, and camping with cousins in the high desert.

When we arrived, My brother and his family were already there. While my husband set up our campsite, we visited with Rick and his family. It was fun to see my brother's new tent trailer decorated with lights, a colorful tablecloth, and a coffee counter with all the fixings. We visited until bedtime and made plans for the weekend.

The next morning, the kids and I went to Rick's campsite while my husband made breakfast. We had a cup of coffee while the kids talked excitedly about the day.

Right after breakfast, the kids wanted to go swimming. So we headed back to our campsite to put on bathing suits. When we got there, we found my husband packing down our campsite. We were shocked and upset. He said the camp host told him someone complained about our beagle barking. If we didn't take care of it, we would have to leave. My husband decided we were going to leave, without talking to me, without discussing it. I couldn't believe it.

I said, "No, stop. I'll go talk to the camp host. We don't *have* to go."

Still, my husband insisted that we were leaving and not to talk to the camp host. I was already on my way there when I heard him order the children into the van. Of course, the camp host said we did not have to leave. So I went to our van and explained; everything was going to be fine. But his mind was set, he said we were leaving and demanded that I get in the van. I once again repeated, pleading, "No, we don't *have* to leave."

Suddenly, he took off in the van, with the kids screaming and crying inside.

He was already on the highway. I started sprinting, I ran hard and far to catch up. A sense of desperation filled my mind; panic pounded in my heart. *What was he doing? What was he **going** to do?* My mind raced, thinking of the fearsome possibilities. At the same time, I was problem solving. My brother couldn't fit both his family and my family in his car. We were three hours from home. My chest was heaving as I fought to catch up to my children. He finally pulled the van over, and I got into the passenger seat.

I did not have a chance to ask him to turn around and start over. Instead, he yelled at me about not being a submissive wife. The three-hour car ride home was silent. I sat in the front seat, quietly questioning whether I was a submissive wife or not: *I want to honor God. I want to lead my husband to the Lord by my good behavior. Had*

I done wrong? What are the kids feeling and thinking? I just wish we could be back with my brother. I wish we could get out of this van.

When we got home from the campsite, my husband went straight to bed, even though it was mid-day. He left the van for me and the kids to unload, as if being snatched away from the fun camping trip wasn't punishment enough. That night, our street had a block party for the Fourth of July. My husband would not get out of bed. The kids and I made the best of our night. We enjoyed the evening with our friends, each of us wishing we were back with family still camping.

Reflection

I didn't find out until later, the reason my husband pulled over was because the kids had hatched a plan to jump out. They slid the side door open, ready to jump because they thought they were being kidnapped. They were terrified.

Rick and his family experienced my husband's rash actions first-hand that day. They stood helplessly aside, wondering if they should call the police; fear and dread enveloped them, and then we disappeared.

I think back on that day with heartache. I grieve the loss of the fun memories we had planned with my brother and his family. I am sad for the absolute fear and desperation my children and I felt.

Even today, I question why I didn't leave him then. But the lie, that I was not being a submissive enough wife, had taken root. Ephesians 5:22–24 says, "Wives submit yourselves to your own husbands as you do to the Lord. For the husband is the head of the wife as Christ is head of the church." At that time, I did not have an accurate understanding of this scripture. It was not until years later that I understood he was using this scripture out of context to manipulate me, deflecting his own wrongdoing.

I now know my husband was the one not following scripture.

I had experienced every type of abuse from this man, who was supposed to love me more than he loved himself. He did not love his wife as Christ loved the church. Ephesians 5:26–27 gives a picture of how a husband must love and treat his wife: "Husbands, love your wives, just as Christ loved the church and gave himself up for her ... and to present her to himself as radiant ... without stain or ... blemish, but holy and blameless."

Christ sacrificed Himself for the church. Husbands should strive to be selfless in their love for their wives, investing time with them. A wife is not owned by her husband and does not exist for his comfort, happiness, and service. A husband should be supportive, encouraging his wife's natural talents and abilities. He should help her to thrive so she can help and serve her family, friends, and community.

As the leader or head of the home, the husband's purifying love is seen in the way he leads spiritually. 1 Peter 3:7 states that the prayers of a husband will be hindered if he is not being respectful of his wife, treating her as a fellow heir of God's grace. The husband should be respectful and considerate, treating his wife as a fellow heir, a partner in grace.

Many women, including me, initially cringe at the phrase "Wives be submissive to your husbands." It conjures the image of cowering and relinquishing what makes you a unique person. This submission, as explained in 1 Peter 3:1, is given out of devotion and love to the Lord. This submission is more akin to teamwork, where members submit to one another according to their gifts, strengths, and abilities. Let's remember verse 5:21 of Ephesians that starts, "Submit to one another out of reverence for Christ." Our whole focus is to be out of reverence for Christ.

So I would encourage you to do as Colossians 3:23 says: "Work willingly at whatever you do, as though you were working for the Lord rather than for people" (NLT). That includes working at our marriages. Instead of being reactionary in your day, ask for God's guidance to respond in respect and love.

If you feel like you have been or are being abused spiritually in any of your relationships, ask yourself if they are using scripture to help you or control you, to encourage you, or to justify their actions?

If you think scripture is being used to intimidate or manipulate you, take time to read that scripture in context. If you are unclear about how you or others should respond to that scripture, pray to the Holy Spirit and seek His help. Read Bible commentaries and resources that address that scripture. Ask a pastor or ministry leader you trust to help you study. If you suspect a spiritual concept is being used to control or confine you, ask that person for more information. Where are they getting that idea? Can they give you another scripture that connects to this idea? Let the resources mentioned above help you reframe scripture or concepts in the light that God intended.

If you do not feel comfortable sharing new biblical understanding for fear of confrontation, remember you have established that truth in your own mind and heart. So when scripture is used wrongly against you, you know you are safe and protected, by repeating the truth in your mind.

Intimacy: Sexual Abuse

I can't explain it, but I could *feel* when my husband had pornographic magazines in the house. I remember one time, I found a stash while he was at work. I was so angered, so insulted, and so disgusted. It happened to be garbage night in our neighborhood. I got in the car with his stash and started depositing different magazines in other people's garbage cans. I regret that lack of forethought and hope it did not cause problems to anyone. All I was thinking about was ridding my home of this filth.

Once when doing the laundry, I found a phone number. I called it, only to find it belonged to a dancer at a strip club. I kindly explained who I was and said I was trying desperately to save my marriage. I asked her to please stop any contact with my husband. She apologized, and that was the end of our conversation.

Sometimes, my husband would suggest ideas for us to try in the bedroom. I would because I thought this way, he wouldn't feel the need to go elsewhere. I drew the line at interacting with other men or couples. In fact, the thought that he wanted me to engage sexually with others deeply hurt.

One time when he was gone on a business trip, he called home, asking me to find his Day-Timer. I went to his office, in our basement and instead found printed emails of explicit content with another woman. I also found some very raunchy and sexually violent sites he visited on the computer. I was livid. I got branch cutters and cut the cords to the computer. The kids and I were to pick him up at the airport that night but I was done. We were leaving him!

So while the kids were in school, I began loading our things in the van. I called his best friend and asked if he could please pick him up from the airport and explained that something had come up. The last thing I loaded into the van was Will's little mattress. I slammed the back doors of the van and then paused; after praying, I felt prompted to stay. I called his friend and said I would be able to pick him up after all. I unloaded the van and put everything back before the kids got home.

When we picked him up at the airport, I was still livid but wanted to be careful with the kids around. He knew I was hopping mad. I said simply that I had found things in his office and we needed to talk. When we got home and the kids were in bed, we went to the basement, and I let him have it. I was furious. I showed him what I'd done to the computer. I read the emails aloud and told him he needed help.

I think he was surprised that I finally blew my stack. He said I was right and that he would stop. For days, there was nothing to talk about. I had lost all respect for him. The only hope I had for our marriage was through the Lord's intervention. It was only through the power of the Holy Spirit that I was able to stay, that I was able to unload that van, to pick him up at the airport, and to give him one more chance to get his act together.

27

Reflection

"Sexual abuse in marriage is not something that is readily disclosed or discussed. It feels shameful to admit even to one's self that your own husband treats you as if your sole purpose is to provide him your body whenever and however, he wants sex. But that is not God's intent for her as a woman or as a wife. God designed the sexual relationship in marriage to reflect a sacred oneness of unselfishness, safety and love."

Regardless of whether your spouse is a Christian or not, they do not own you or your body. 1 Corinthians 7:4 says, "The wife does not have authority over her own body but yields it to her husband." My husband used to say this and then say, "I own you. I can do whatever I want with you."

Reading this verse in context helps us understand God's meaning. 1 Corinthians 7:2–7 says, "But since sexual immorality is occurring, each man should have sexual relations with his own wife, and each woman with her own husband. The husband should fulfill his marital duty to his wife, and likewise the wife to her husband. The wife does not have authority over her own body but yields it to her husband. *In the same way, the husband does not have authority over his own body but yields it to his wife*" (emphasis mine).

In reality, this whole passage speaks to equality in marriage. Both husband and wife are responsible for keeping their marriage pure and maintaining their marital vows. Couples should maintain faithfulness in a transparent, vulnerable, intimate relationship. This way, husband and wife are content, not only in physical intimacy but all aspects of marriage: mental, emotional, and spiritual.

Honestly, it takes vigilant work to maintain this trust, demonstrating intimacy in every aspect. We must protect our spouses from temptation by doing the hard work of keeping that bond of unity. It takes maturity to not let your devotion in marriage hinge on your emotions in the moment. Your wedding vow is for all time, regardless of arguments and differences of opinion.

1 Corinthians 7:5 says, "Do not deprive each other except perhaps by mutual consent and for a time, so that you may devote yourselves to prayer. Then come together again so that Satan will not tempt you because of your lack of self-control. I say this as a concession, not as a command."

Corinthians also speaks against spouses who may use sexual, marital intimacy as something to be earned or withdrawn as punishment or a power play. Sexual intimacy with your spouse is meant to be an expression of your bond, your love, and your appreciation for one another. It is to be a loving, joyous, passionate act shared mutually between both husband and wife, strengthening your relationship.

I was a stay-at-home mom and had to mentally transition from maintaining the household, seeing to the kid's needs, and so on, to turn toward intimacy. My mind was juggling a million thoughts at once: did I sign the permission slip for the field trip tomorrow, do we have enough milk for morning? I explained to my husband that it was equivalent to me showing up at his business meeting and wanting him to put all that aside so we could be intimate. The home was my office. I needed time to make that mental shift. It could be as simple as him putting the kids to bed or sprucing up the bedroom to set the mood. This allowed me to take a shower to reset and make myself feel desirable.

Much of a woman's ability to be open in the area of intimate sexuality stems from her self-confidence and the feeling she is appealing to her husband. If she feels valued, she will be more open to an engaging, close physical relationship. If there was a misunderstanding or argument, there may still be resentment to address before a wife can put herself in a loving, vulnerable, passionate mindset.

With all of this in mind, sexual intimacy is also not meant to be a selfish act. Maybe you are in a marriage where your spouse wants you to try things you are not comfortable with, including looking at pornographic material, sharing your intimate acts with others, or trying new things that may be hurtful. Maybe you feel they want to do something that is not in line with scripture or righteous living. If this is true, you have every right to say no. First of all, your body belongs to God. Your body is not meant for sexual immorality but for the Lord, as stated in 1 Corinthians 6:13. Second, you can simply tell your spouse you do not feel comfortable participating in whatever it may be. It may be helpful to get couples counseling to work out differences in sexual expectations and improve communication.

I would encourage you not to compare your sexual intimacy with others or with magazine articles, talk shows, or any other form of report. God created sex. He designed it to be a beautiful, loving, and pleasurable experience. So it is right to pray for purity, for faithfulness, and for God to help you be in the mood. Your focus should be what makes you and your spouse feel fulfilled in this form of intimacy.

The Goat

Our backyard was in bad shape. It was early spring, and I had asked my husband to take care of it, but he never did. It was fenced in, a perfect place for kids to play safely, but because of neglect, it was getting overrun with weeds and thorny blackberry bushes.

I saw an ad in the paper selling a female pygmy goat; I called the number, and the farmer agreed to meet in the Walmart parking lot that night. After the kids were put to bed, I excused myself from the house, stating I needed to buy some milk. I went to Walmart, bought the milk, and pulled around back, where I exchanged cash for a black, gray, and white female goat. She bordered on rotund, and I hoisted her into the back of the van and slipped into the driver's seat.

As I adjusted my tan trench coat around me, I heard a small voice from the back say, "Cool, Mom."

Startled, I turned around to find a stowaway in the back seat.

Ryan, my youngest, had followed me out to the van and hidden in the back seat. He had apparently sensed something stealthy afoot and positioned himself to be in on the covert plan. I swore him to secrecy until morning.

The next morning, the kids were delighted to find our new pet in the backyard. She came with the name Cinder, but my kids quickly renamed her Willow.

My husband was shocked and a little amused. She did her job and helped get our backyard into shape.

The kids loved having a goat. She was a sweet and fun backyard companion for them. We got her a leash and collar, and the kids enjoyed walking her down our neighborhood sidewalks. I am sure Willow enjoyed the love and attention she got as she was paraded around the neighborhood. We were the only family in our Portland neighborhood to have a goat (no surprise there).

One late fall Sunday, as the kids and I returned home from church, we entered through the backyard gate to find Willow was gone. Alarmed, the kids went tearing through the back door, asking their dad if he'd seen Willow. Had she gotten out of the fence? He coolly responded that he'd gotten rid of her.

He explained he drove her out to the country and gave her to some stranger. We were shocked, hurt, and heartbroken. He had just ripped her out of our lives with no warning and no consideration of anyone's feelings.

However, this was not our last experience with a pet goat. Years later, when the boys were in middle school, we rented an old farmhouse in the country. While living there, we got a baby goat from a friend who raised milk goats. Male goats were of no use to them. We named him Levi. He was a beloved nuisance as he grew. He was funny, smart, and sometimes infuriating. Ryan loved to play with Levi. As the goat grew, Ryan would roughhouse with him. Levi would attempt to rear up and butt Ryan, and my son would leap out of the way and then push Levi away, only to have the goat come at him again.

Also, this goat learned to open car doors with his mouth; many times, he would greet me at my car when I came home from work and open the door for me. By this time, my kids were driving, and I had to remind them to lock their car doors so Levi wouldn't get in.

When Ryan was in high school, he had a job at a local department store. He had the habit of putting his paycheck in his visor until he got to the bank to deposit it. However, one time, Ryan had an unfortunate experience: Levi got into his car and ate his paycheck; after that, he locked his car doors when parked in our driveway.

Reflection

Memories, both good and bad, form who we become. The kids and I were helpless in the loss of our dear pet Willow. It was thoughtless and hurtful for my husband to get rid of her, and it added another layer to the wall of distrust.

I read once that the way children first process grief sets the template for how they will process grief moving forward in life. Looking back, it would have been wise to initiate a grieving time that reminded us of good memories of Willow.

Many times, as parents, we forget our children are individuals with growing hearts, minds, characters, and personalities. Their days are affected by our thoughtful behaviors and words (or the lack thereof). We need to let them know we value their perspective and how they feel about circumstances or life events (like a pet suddenly being taken away).

It's important to take time to relish those good days and process the sad ones. Help your kids learn to retell their stories and experiences. It teaches them a healthy way to process and shape who they are becoming.

Jesus values children. There are so many verses that express that in the Bible. Mark 10:14–16 says, "When Jesus saw this, he was indignant. He said to them, 'Let the little children come to me, and do not hinder them, for the kingdom of God belongs to such as these. Truly I tell you, anyone who will not receive the kingdom of God like a little child will never enter it.'"

We must welcome God, communicate with Him, learn about His plans with the mindset and heart of a child. The only way to do this is to learn how children communicate with and welcome God into their lives.

I have a small book called *Children's Letters to God*. The letters show how honest kids are and how they think about and communicate with God. Here are a few examples:

> This one must have come from the Pacific Northwest: "Why can't you keep it from raining on Saturday all the time?"
>
> —Rose

> "Dear God, if you do all these things, you are pretty busy. Now here's my question. When is the best time I can talk to you? I know you are always listening but when will you be listening hard in Troy, New York?"
>
> —Sincerely yours, Allen

> "Dear God, I just feel good knowing that you are everywhere. That's all."
>
> —Respectfully, Margaret

> "Dear God, I am sorry I was late for Sunday school but I couldn't find my underwear."
>
> —Norman

> "Dear God, sometimes I am very scared in my room at night. I know you are there to protect me."
>
> —Your friend, Diane

"Dear God, when it didn't rain, I was sure my violets would not grow. But then it came up. What you did was pretty good."

—Love, Betty

What I love about these letters is the familiar way the kids approach God about everyday things. They do not take for granted that He is there, that He cares about their daily adventures, and that it matters to Him.

This is true not just of children but all of us. We can have these open, ongoing interactions with Him as we walk through our day; whether it is gray or sunny, He is listening. We can model this for our kids, but guess what? If you are tuned in, you will see; they model it for us, as well.

Protecting Him at My Cost

One evening, just after saying goodnight, my husband leaned over and kissed me, then he suddenly tried to suffocate me with a pillow. I squirmed out but he grabbed my neck and began to strangle me. I thought, *What's happening? He's trying to kill me!*

I got loose and ran as fast as I could to the bathroom. Once inside, I tried to slam the door shut. But his shoulder shoved the door, throwing me back on the floor. He was in a rage and began to hit me. After he'd exhausted himself, I lay quietly on the bathroom floor, and he stalked out. When I was sure the coast was clear, I got to my hands and knees, and crawled to the girls' bedroom. They were sound asleep, thankfully unaware of what just happened. I was dumbfounded by his rampage and had no idea what triggered it. Trembling, I lay awake on my back on their bedroom floor. I was in shock and terrified.

The next morning, when I came into the dining room, I saw he had cut the phone lines (at the time, we only had landlines). I was scared; we were trapped. I got the girls breakfast while my mind raced about what to do. After a while, he came in from outside and apologized. I asked why he exploded, trying to kill me. He claimed I had made a face when he kissed me. It was pitch-dark in the room; even if I had made a face, he couldn't have seen it. Now, he was being sweet and coddling. He brought me a bouquet of flowers and said he would buy new lines and fix the phones later that day. I was extremely wary. My mind was still racing, but his behavior, words, and attitude seemed to reflect remorse.

Sometimes, as in this instance, there was no visible tension building, or maybe he had tension building inside, and I was unaware of it. The next day, he made excuses for his behavior, attempting to lavish care and attention on me, but inside, I was cautious. The honeymoon phase kicked in; things were calm for quite a while, and I let my guard down in an attempt to resume a normal life.

Over the years, there were many instances where the children and I experienced his angry outbursts. Physical aggression was primarily directed at me and usually took the form of choking, shoving me, or pinning me against a wall.

In another incident, years later, I had loaded and started the dishwasher, then left the kitchen. But the dishwasher started leaking. Water and suds poured out and apparently dripped into my husband's office in the basement. He roared up the stairs, yelling and calling me names I will not repeat here. I had no idea what was going on. As I rounded the corner, I saw the water and suds pouring out of the dishwasher. Demanding that I clean this mess up, he stormed back downstairs to his office. I went to get towels from the linen closet.

After he went back downstairs, I was angry and locked the basement door. I intended to unlock it after I'd finished cleaning up, but he heard the lock click. In anger, he scrambled through one of the basement windows and then barreled through the front door. Just at that moment, I took a business call on our wall phone in the kitchen. He took the receiver with his left hand and grabbed my throat with his right.

He held me there while he took the call, squeezing ever tighter. Shoved against the kitchen wall, I was suspended in his grip. I could not make a sound but was screaming inside. After he hung up, he let go of my throat and tore into me verbally. He said I had brought this upon myself, then he went back to work. I sat, stunned and in pain.

The next day was a Christmas tea at church. I got all dressed up and picked up my mom. The sanctuary was beautifully and festively decorated. Large circular tables draped with satiny white cloth filled the room. Candlelit centerpieces of red, green, and gold accented with pine set the stage for the delicate petit fours and other dainty treats on our table. As the tea progressed, I found that I could not open my mouth to enjoy the many wonderful treats. I was in a considerable amount of pain. I apologized and told my mom that I was feeling sick and needed to go. After I dropped her off, I went straight to the emergency room. The doctors explained I had the equivalent to the mumps and gave me pain medicine. They asked how this happened and of course, I made up some lies. Why? I was still protecting him, protecting my family.

Reflection

I was protecting him at my cost. I was endlessly hopeful that he would give his heart and life over to the Lord. I hoped he would stop being abusive, that we would have the marriage I had dreamed of. I worked to be respectful, understanding, supportive, submissive, and compromising. I was patient and long suffering, with a vision that things will eventually work out.

I do not like to take the long way around the bend; I would rather fix things right away. I don't like to let misunderstandings or arguments sit and fester. He preferred to run and hide, not talk anything through and later act like everything was back to normal. This pattern left me feeling frustrated and stymied, uncared for and lonely. There were roadblocks in our journey, with no attempts to repair them. Each moment of abuse, betrayal, and apathy added cracks in our path, potholes in our relationship.

I had committed to him, for better or for worse. I thought, *Is this the "worst" part? The uphill climb of the marriage journey? Is this what those vows meant?*

Without, at least, separation and professional help, abusive behavior will not resolve on its own. If not worked out, the cracks and fissures only grow, changing the path ahead for children and possibly through the generations.

If you are experiencing abuse, you are not invisible to God. He sees the road you're on; if you invite Him, you will not walk it alone. Recall to mind the journey of Joseph. He suffered mistreatment, false accusations, and punishment from the time he was a teen through his imprisonment as an adult. Yet, he chose to include God in his broken journey, holding onto God's faithfulness.

Through unfair circumstances, God led Joseph to exactly where he needed to be for His plans to come about. In Genesis 50, Joseph has the opportunity to confront his brothers; he says in Genesis 50:20, "You intended to harm me, but God intended it for good … the saving of many lives." God turned the unjust path of Joseph's journey into mercy for many.

You, your children, your circumstances are not invisible to God. He never intended you to suffer from the words or actions of the one who is supposed to love you. In these times when you feel alone and there is no one to turn to and no words to pray, just cry out to God in your mind. Sometimes, all I could pray was, "Please help." Hebrews 13:5–6 says, "Never will I leave you; never will I forsake you … So, we say with confidence, The Lord is my helper; I will not be afraid." When you are able, take some time alone with God. Ask Him to show you where He is. You may be surprised and relieved to find that He gives you an image of Him standing right beside you, maybe even in front of you, guarding, or maybe He gives you an image of being held in His lap. He has not left you. Put your trust in God; He has a plan. He can guide you through your broken road of sadness, bewilderment, anger, and loneliness. Only God can guide you along a path toward beautiful healing and hope.

Sprinkling Salt

Salt absorbs into everything; it becomes part of a dish until it is not distinguishable. You are aware of its presence and how it alters the dish, but you can't take the salt out once it is absorbed. Emotional, psychological, and verbal abuse can be like sprinkling salt into your life.

These forms of abuse were not stand-alone incidents that I could point to. They occurred in such a subtle way that sometimes I didn't even recognize it as demeaning or done with malice. It was our marriage lifestyle.

Recently, I was talking to a woman who also experienced emotional abuse in her marriage. She said, "It happened so subtly. If it had started as harsh and abrupt, I would have been out of there."

Somehow, we resign ourselves to being treated or talked to in that manner. Let's say one time you are called dumb; in your mind, you may reason, *Yeah, that was kind of dumb of me.* You just swallow it. But then it happens again and again. This salt, this abuse that was sprinkled into each day, came in several different forms.

Emotional Abuse and Neglect

Neglect goes hand in hand with emotional abuse. Emotional neglect looks like refusing to spend time with you, preferring to engage in solitary activity. It is the feeling that you are not a priority in your husband's life; he is not intentionally connecting with you and is not willing to listen or discuss your thoughts or ideas, wants, needs, or concerns with you. It leaves you feeling starved for connection.

I had hoped my husband would be there for me, but emotional neglect became the basis for my low self-esteem. It led me to wonder, *What is wrong with me? Why doesn't my husband want to spend time with me or with us as a family?*

I remember whenever I planned an outing with the kids, the morning of the activity, my husband would often say he wasn't going.

Each time, I would try to be the cheerleader, saying, "It will be fun. Once we get there, you'll be so glad you came. I'll pack your favorite food, build memories with the kids." But no matter what I said, he would just tell me to go without him. For several years, he wouldn't attend Thanksgiving or Christmas with us at my brother's or parents' house.

For the most part, I did not let my husband's lack of engagement drag me down. He was the one missing out because the kids and I always went ahead with our plans.

Also, he completely disregarded me when I asked for help. For example, the bathroom sink broke in our one-bathroom rental. This meant all of us had to use the kitchen sink for hand washing and teeth brushing. I suggested a plumber; he adamantly refused and would not allow me to call the landlord. The sink was broken for more than a year and was still not working the day we left.

In addition to this, he was often indifferent to my feelings. When Cheri was a newborn, I was feeling desperately alone. His friends would show up unannounced and want to hang out with him. Acting like he was single, he would go to bars and strip clubs with them. One time, when I clutched his sleeve and begged him to stay home, he laughed, made fun of me, and walked out the door.

My concerns were often minimized or trivialized. Whenever I declared my outright abhorrence of his pornography, he would say I was insecure.

I could never have a serious conversation with him in which my thoughts, concerns, or feelings were considered. I often tried to explain to him that calling me names, engaging in porn, physically abusing me, suggesting that we swing added one more layer of bricks in a wall between us. He just laughed.

Psychological Abuse: Manipulation

This salt can also come in the form of psychological abuse, such as manipulation. One evening, we had all just come home from the laundromat. The kids had just settled into the couch to watch television in the basement. Will was in his special seat in the living room, with plastic bags of clean laundry around him.

Once again, my husband was upset; he locked himself in the bathroom with a shotgun, threatening to commit suicide. Instead of sympathy, I got mad. I knew he was not serious but trying to manipulate me. I said it was really selfish of him to even think of this with the kids around, and who was going to clean up that mess?

I returned to the living room to find William had fallen out of his chair and was face first in one of the bags of laundry. When I reached him, his face was dusky and his lips were blue. I was immediately alarmed and revived him. I held him close. I felt so bad that I was distracted from his care.

I want to make it clear, over the years, my husband threatened suicide or would tell me of suicidal attempts or thoughts. But these were used solely in an attempt to manipulate me and the kids.

Psychological threats like this also included threatening to hurt our dog and threatening to destroy things of importance or value to me or the children. He used threats to control and was intentionally slow in getting to or leaving for something that was important to me.

My husband deflected his behavior, blaming it on someone else; often that was me. At one point, he said it was my fault he had an affair because I was so big and pregnant. Another time, he accused me of cheating and being controlling. But when would I have had the time or the freedom to cheat? What was I possibly in control of?

Verbal Abuse

Verbal abuse goes hand in hand with emotional/psychological abuse; it is often seen in belittling, criticizing, and calling names. I was often called a witch, with a capital B, and sometimes with the "F" word in front of that. I was told I was stupid or dumb. He would correct me and say, "Use a brain." He often would quiz me on trivia or history, usually while we were in the car. He would scoff at how little I knew.

One time, Will got very sick and was in the emergency room. I was with him at the hospital, standing at his side, stroking his head. It was morning, and the TV news droned on. My husband burst through the curtain room divider, seething. He began, "Do you know how much I hate you? Every time there is a report of an accident on the news, I hope it is you." He went on and on, as long as no people were in the room.

I stayed calm. I did not respond and kept my back turned. I had no interest in his rant. All of my thoughts were on my sweet William. I was also astounded that this was his focus while our son was struggling and in pain.

Reflection

I later learned that "emotional abuse is an attempt to control using one or several of these methods: accusations, criticisms, blaming … belittling alone or in front of others—even in a 'joking' manner, using a double standard and trying to make the person feel that they are crazy. Emotional manipulation to feel guilty or shamed into doing what the person wants or emotionally attacked for not doing what they want. Or to take on or feel their personal emotions and concerns as your own."

These forms of abuse became part of married life as I knew it. Sometimes, it felt like I was gingerly walking on top of the snow; other times, I just kicked off the slush. Still the words and actions had their effect on my self-esteem.

Words leave bruises and scars. Years later, those names and impressions would hit my mind hard. His names for me would strike back, and I'd hear in my mind, *You dumb b****.

However, these bruises and scars do not go unnoticed by God. God never hurls labels or accusations. It took time to replace the untrue names and labels with truth from my heavenly Father, such as chosen, loved, redeemed, wonderfully made, accepted, and many more.

Do you have negative labels that have been put on you by friends, family, co-workers, people of authority? Then I would encourage you to sit before the Lord and ask, What names or labels do You give me? Write down what He impresses on you. Turn through scripture to find the truth: Who are you according to God's Word? Keep these truths present in your mind so they can kick off the mud hurled in your path. In time, you will walk through each day in confidence, living loved.

Below are scriptures that helped me relabel myself; hopefully, they can help you as well:

- Friend: "I have called you friends, for everything that I learned from my Father I have made known to you" (John 15:15b).
- Loved, Cared-for, Delighted-in, Protected: "I call on you, my God, for you will answer me; turn your ear to me and hear my prayer. Show me the wonders of your great love, you who save by your right hand those who take refuge in you from their foes. Keep me as the apple of your eye; hide me in the shadow of your wings" (Psalm 17:6–8).
- His Child, His Heir: "So in Christ Jesus you are all children of God through faith" (Galatians 3:26). "Now if we are children, then we are heirs—heirs of God and co-heirs with Christ, if indeed we share in his sufferings in order that we may also share in his glory" (Romans 8:17).

My Daughters

From the moment I found out I was carrying a little one inside me, my heart intertwined with my baby. As I held each child in my arms, I was filled with an overwhelming sense of love. A mother's love has no finality; it grows with the seasons, the years.

When I look at each of my children, I see all that they are, all that they have been, and all that lies ahead. My heart is warmed with memories of them as infants, toddlers, and self-assured preschoolers. My heart is overjoyed with memories of elementary kids as they discovered life, schooling, and friendships. I burst with pride as I remember each accomplishment as they discovered their interests in middle school and high school.

Each of my children's personalities and journeys are an important part of my own. I am aware the path you are reading about was not walked alone. My children walked it as well, growing up along the way. No matter the bright perspective I worked to portray; my children still absorbed the distress of the abuse I experienced. I reasoned that staying, I could protect them and keep them safe. This way, they would never experience a custody battle or be home alone with my husband. On the other hand, I was aware that exposure to emotional, mental, and physical abuse would seep into their character development.

I finally understood that I did not want my girls growing up thinking this was the kind of man they should look for in a spouse. Below is a character sketch of each of my three oldest, my three daughters:

My Oldest: Marion

Marion had big feelings coursing through her small body. My daughter was contemplative, introspective, very much in tune with her feelings. She needed time to process. It was fascinating to watch her evaluate her surroundings. As a toddler, nothing missed her inspection; every flower, bug, bird, butterfly, she pointed out or remarked on.

When she started elementary school, she had an uncanny ability to pick up on the emotions of peers and adults. She could zone into a hurt heart with sweetness, kind words, a hand on a shoulder, or sitting close by. She could easily sense my frustration or worry and attempted to voice what I was processing.

When my sweet daughter was in the fifth grade, her dad said something that broke her heart. She cried all the way to school. We stopped outside her classroom door. I coached her to take a deep breath, suck up her tears, and head into class. I told her the rest of the day would be better. Looking back, I wish I had whisked her off for a special time with me. Each mom has moments of regret, but those moments are by far outweighed by treasured times of joy, laughter, moments of heartfelt discussions, and prayers.

To this day, Marion remains sensitive, thoughtful, imaginative, and observant. Due to her younger brother's hospitalizations and operations, she has a very sensitive heart toward children with medical needs. From late elementary on, she was determined to become a pediatric neurosurgeon. Marion is now working in the medical field. She is dedicated to helping kids improve and succeed. I am proud to see her heart for helping others.

Second Oldest: Kay

Growing up, Kay was a spark, a spitfire. She was full of whimsy, dreams, passion, and curiosity. Practically everyone she met was a friend. When I think of Kay, I often think of the song from *The Sound of Music*, "How Do You Solve a Problem Like Maria?" She was so caught up in life, like Maria.

By preschool, she had no trouble speaking her mind and standing for what was right. As she was drying her hands at a restroom mall, she observed a woman walk out without washing her hands. She went running after her, shouting, "Ma'am, you forgot to wash your hands."

She was a champion for the underdog. She exuded confidence and a mind for justice. Kay once asked me if it cost money to get a job because she wanted to help the homeless people standing on the corner.

Kay was also a voracious reader. In fact, I as a consequence of behavior, I kept her from reading, as that was her greatest pastime. One day, she was supposed to be preparing dinner for the family. I was upstairs and heard the smoke alarm go off. I ran downstairs to see the microwave and kitchen cabinets over the stove in flames. Kay had become so caught up in her book that she completely forgot about the pot on the stove.

Today, Kay is a new mom to an infant and toddler daughters; she's also an preschoolteacher. She is surely teaching her students the joy of reading.

Youngest: Cheri

Cheri was an introvert, not talkative and very much a go-with-the-flow kind of gal. She shared her room, her clothes, her food, and just about everything else, except for candy. My quiet girl saved candy like she was rationing for the Great Depression. She had boxes and drawers with candy tucked inside.

Cheri was a goal setter. When she was four years old, she saw a kid down the street with a Little Tykes car. She saved every coin she found, scoured her dad's pockets, tucked away birthday and gift money. By the time she was five, she had saved up enough money. We took her to the store, and she test-drove every toy car in her price range. It was a proud purchase, and I admired her for being that determined, persistent, and focused.

Cheri had to work harder for her grades than her sisters. She had a difficult third grade teacher who seemed biased against her. She really didn't enjoy school but was persistent despite the extra effort.

Despite her struggles in school as a child, she was the first of my kids to receive her master's degree, and she is now an excellent third grade teacher. To this day, she has a sizable candy stash and was the first of my kids to buy her own home.

Reflection

Each of my daughters is uniquely distinct and delightful. Because of their individual attributes, I enjoy specific activities with each of them. With Marion, I've gone to symphonies, ballets, live theater, and operas. With Kay, I've enjoyed lively conversations, sharing dreams and goals, and discussing books and how to make the world better over coffee. With Cheri, I enjoy shopping, watching basketball games, eating out together, and movies, and sharing the humor and heartache of working with elementary students.

I take great pleasure in each of my daughters' personality traits and preferences. Each of my daughters are superb bakers and cooks. We've enjoyed preparing meals and treats together. They also all have compassionate, caring hearts for others, desiring to help people and make a difference.

I continually learn from and admire my girls. My heart aches with theirs when they go through hard times, and I rejoice over their accomplishments; we've laughed and cried together through it all.

My Sons

A mother's love transforms as each child grows up, even as they start their adult lives. If a bond is broken, a mother's love does not break; it changes and transforms. It does not end.

My children's personalities and journeys are an important part of my own. Each child contributes a facet to the family paragon. Each provides a contrasting glint supplementing in richness and depth to the other members.

No matter my positive perspective, my children absorbed the distress of the abuse I experienced. I finally understood that I did not want my boys to grow up thinking my ex-husband was the kind of man they should become. As I wrote about my girls, I want to share a glimpse of my three youngest, my three sons.

Oldest: William

After three months in the NICU, Will left the hospital the day before Thanksgiving, a day of special gratitude, accompanied by a heart and lung monitor. This alarm would go off whenever there was a life-threatening situation.

Will was born with cerebral palsy; he is a nonverbal quadriplegic, and we feed him through a g-tube. He was a delight and was deeply impacted by music. Although he was nonverbal, he could understand much of what was said by others and communicated with his eyes, his laughter, his vocalizations, his smiles, and his tears. He had the most beautiful eyelashes and a sweet laugh. He loved balloons, bubbles, and the color hot pink. He liked bumpy rides in his wheelchair and the feeling of rain on his face. Hearing words that rhyme and someone reading off lists made him laugh.

Yet, he had many medical challenges, which led to numerous surgeries and hospital stays. The sights, smells, and sounds of the hospitals and medical equipment were common as we spent hours and days there over the course of Will's life. The hospitals during the holidays were special. At Christmas, hundreds of leather-clad motorcyclists would roar up the big hill to the Shriner's Hospital, loaded with gifts for patients and their siblings. At Easter, there were Easter baskets and festive candies. Embedded in our family memories are extended hospital stays.

William loved going to school, and everything we did as a family, he did. We went camping and hiking, went out to restaurants and movies, went on picnics, went to the beach, everything. One summer, I asked the kids if they would like to take a camping trip without Will. He could stay in a facility for a long weekend, or someone could care for him at home. They wouldn't hear of it. They wouldn't dream of doing any family activities without him.

Will enriched our lives in very personal and individual ways. We experienced joy in the midst of uncertainty, hardship, and pain. Our hope and faith expanded through Will. Empathy and compassion are rooted in each of Will's siblings because of the life shared with their brother Will.

Second Oldest: Thomas

Due to Will's complications, extra precautions were taken with Thomas. Thomas's delivery was normal. However, his body rejected his own blood due to distress Will suffered in my womb. Thomas was taken to the NICU for transfusions and he had to be wrapped in a blanket of lights. I had to leave the hospital with empty arms once again. Thankfully short days later, Thomas came home, a wonderful healthy baby, ready to be enveloped into the fold.

From the time Thomas learned to walk, he ran. His sweet face was always full of smiles and expectation at the start of each day.

At kindergarten graduation, his teacher faced the room and said, "I want you all to remember this guy's name. Great things are going to come from this guy." To this day, I believe this to be true.

As he grew, his reputation for being kind, caring, and thoughtful preceded him. Thomas would observe a need, in any setting, at camp, at church, at school, or at home, and readily jump in to help.

In high school, jobs were hard to come by, so he started his own catering business. He made up a menu of a number of items that he prepared for families and delivered them hot. He was hired to cater elders' meetings, weddings, and other events. No matter what job he has taken, Thomas has quickly risen to the top. He has a strong work ethic, with innate leadership skills and high emotional intelligence, allowing him to connect well with staff and customers.

Thomas held a management position in the food service industry and is very skilled in leading and encouraging a team.

Youngest: Ryan

By preschool, Ryan was ready to be a grown-up and thought of himself as one. He would get dressed, get his little briefcase, and say he had a business meeting. I watched as he stood at the bus stop on the corner. After a few minutes, he would come back, saying,

"My meeting was canceled." Frequently, as we drove around town, he would declare, "See that bridge [or skyscraper], I built that," as though it were true.

Ryan was a take-charge kind of kid. When he was four, my mom and I talked about childcare for him while everyone else was at school. Overhearing our conversations, he took it upon himself to call the "regulars," notifying them that he needed someone to stay with him.

From quite young, he felt called to ministry. He was very matter of fact in his declarations, and sometimes his siblings would give him a hard time. When he was six, he was very hurt and frustrated that his siblings did not take him seriously when discussing the Bible. He ran outside; I found him across the street at a fenced-in preschool playground. He said God had told him he was going to be a pastor. I talked with him about the story of Joseph. When Joseph tried to share visions God had given him of leadership, his brothers got angry (Genesis 37–50). I told him I believed what God had laid on his heart but that it would take time and patience.

Throughout high school, he volunteered at a Bible camp, doing everything from maintenance to being a camp counselor. He was willing to do any task asked without grumbling or complaining. Ryan demonstrated wisdom, diligently seeking out godly male mentors who taught him many skills, including building maintenance and automotive repair.

He and his wife met in middle school; she happens to be the youngest of six in her family too. Today, he is a father of an infant and toddler boy, an associate pastor at a local church, responsible for the youth and college ministry, and he preaches monthly.

Reflection

My sons are distinctly different. Ryan invests deeply with a few: those he mentors, and those he works with at church and in university. Thomas loves interacting with everyone, excited to meet and spend time with friends and acquaintances. Thomas and I enjoy taking outings to the coast. With Ryan, I enjoy doing acts of service. Both of my sons are excellent cooks and bakers.

My Children

My children often came to me in exasperation, saying, "Why can't [sibling] be more like me?" I would respond that God wired each of them differently. Respect and try to admire your differences because God will use them in a different way than He will use you. There are seasons and even days when you connect with one child more than another. But whenever my kids asked, "Who is your favorite?" I would respond something like, "You are all my favorites. There are characteristics about each of you that I love and admire." And it is true.

I became a student of each of my children, infusing God-directed creativity, joy, flexibility, and faith in their lives. I recognized and cultivated their strengths, natural interests, and abilities. I made an effort to observe, connect, and approach each child based on their preferences and needs.

I learned to be intentional about speaking words of affirmation, listing the strengths I admired and their abilities in certain areas. Even in providing corrections, I found sandwiching a negative between two positives was the best approach.

I reveled in hearing their thoughts, ideas, plans, and sense of humor. I enjoyed being on the fringes of conversations and activities with their friends. These times not only deepened our relationship and shared community but also gave me insight into how they ticked.

Raising a family as individuals and as a unit is difficult and a constant learning process. My children are all adults now, and I am still learning how to honor them, allow for their choices, and respect them despite disagreeing with some of their decisions. I trust God, even now, in their continued growth, my growth, and the legacy of our family.

I often stumbled and fell in parenting; I flat-out bombed at times. But I continually seek God and ask Him to provide me with discernment, insight, wisdom, and creativity. I look to Him to show me ways to reach and teach my kids individually and as a group.

I encourage you to study your children, look at them as individuals, and really get to know their strengths and weaknesses. Discover their learning style, their love language, how their birth order impacts them. Doing these things can maximize guidance, relationships, and influence in their self-esteem.

Most important is Proverbs 3:5–6: "Trust in the Lord with all your heart and do not lean on your own understanding. In all your ways acknowledge Him and He will make straight your paths." Pray for God to enlighten you in your parenting so you can see beyond the surface and act beyond the immediate. When your kids face difficult circumstances due to their own choices or the bumps and bruises of daily life, trust God to use those twists and turns as their story in Him. Take heart in God's sovereignty with regards to the legacy of your family. Trust Him to complete His work for each of your children.

Why Did I Stay?

Thinking back on my abusive experiences, I often wondered, why did I stay? (Others have wondered that too.) It has to do with the reconciliation/honeymoon phase of the abuse cycle. My husband wasn't always angry or abusive. We had good times. I saw potential in him, which gave me hope for our marriage.

I wanted to believe my marriage could work, and I was determined to do my part. I protected his reputation because I hoped and prayed he would change. I misunderstood my responsibility.

Although he was treating me wrong, I believed it was my job to make our family work. At one point, he agreed to counseling with a pastor. Just before we got out of the car at the first session, he looked at me and said, "We are not going to discuss the abuse." Needless to say, the counseling did us no good.

As a Christian, I did not see divorce as an option. The number one reason was the verse in 1 Peter 3:1 (NIV): "Wives, in the same way submit yourselves to your own husbands so that, if any of them do not believe the word, they may be won over without words by the behavior of their wives." I had been weighed down with spiritual abuse and did not understand the context of this scripture or its true meaning.

I knew that in raising children, the mom and dad should have a united front. I wanted to do right by him, by the children, and of course by God. However, there were times when my husband's discipline of the children seemed over the line. When I tried to intervene, he would fling accusations against me. One time, after I experienced another incident of physical abuse, I gathered up the kids to leave. My husband snatched up our three-year-old daughter and said I could leave, but not with her. I was not going to have a tug of war with my daughter, and I was not going to leave her behind. So I resigned myself to stay. Still, when thinking about a separation or divorce, I anguished over having to split parenting time. How could I leave my kids with someone I did not feel safe with? I thought at least in staying, I would be able to buffer and protect them.

Reflection

I want to make it clear: Any form of abuse is wrong. If after reading my stories, you believe you are experiencing any form of abuse (physical, spiritual, psychological, or verbal), do not keep silent as I did. Please do not try to protect the abuser's reputation; that will never lead to change. Abuse needs professional intervention to break the cycle, to bring healing, to maintain accountability over time.

Reconciliation cannot take place without professional support. Even then, circumstances may not improve with intervention. If the abuse cycle continues with no consistent change, then reconciliation may not be an option. If so, it is best for the abuser to be removed from the victim and their children immediately. This is necessary until significant counseling, anger management, mentoring, and change is demonstrated, not just given lip service.

Careful planning is best before domestic abuse is brought to light. When an abuser is exposed, the abuse may worsen. Anonymity is a criminal's friend. Abuse is a criminal act. When criminals are exposed, they either run or fight. They may also try to discredit their accuser, hoping to cover their crimes and save face. Abuse is done at the expense of the victim. A fight to elude exposure will be done at the expense of the victim as well. Protection of the victim and kids is the utmost priority.

Sometimes, it's necessary to have a restraining order delivered by the police; follow through. I did not follow through three separate times, out of reluctance and fear. Have a police officer present while they gather their things to leave the home or, if necessary, while you gather your things to leave. Remember who is the perpetrator of harm here; you and your kids need to run from harm to safety.

If you find counseling and intervention are not helping, then it may be time to separate yourself from the abuser. Think about what I have said; learn from my experiences. Read on to find out how I moved toward healing and peace for myself and for my family.

Psalm 138:3 says, "When I called, you answered me; you made me bold and stouthearted." Know that God will strengthen you and hold you up. You can trust in Him and hide in Him as you do what is best for yourself and your family. Zephaniah 3:17 (NASB) says, "The Lord your God is in your midst, a victorious warrior. He will rejoice over you with joy, He will be quiet with His love." In the midst of your suffering, know that God is a mighty warrior in your midst, fighting for you and protecting you through all you endure.

The Bear

In the Pacific Northwest, we spend a lot of time outside, walking through the woods, exploring the beauty of creation, and even camping in the wilderness.

One time, when my kids were ages three to ten, I took them on a camping adventure. We usually camped in our big tent, but this time, we stayed in a three-sided cabin. The front was completely open: no wall nor door, just a few steps leading into a big wooden room with mattress-less bunk beds.

Our first evening, we were warned to bury leftovers far from our cabin, as a black bear had been spotted recently.

That night, as my children slept, I lay awake, reading by flashlight. Just as I turned off my light to go to sleep, I heard a loud, deep huffing sound. I froze.

For a long time, I lay still, listening intently for the sound. I heard nothing and convinced myself I had imagined it. Then the sound came again, louder and longer. I knew it was not my imagination.

My bed was at the front of the cabin opening. I turned on my stomach and peered into the pitch black of night. I lay propped on my forearms with the flashlight off. I thought if I had to, I could quickly turn on the light and frighten the bear away.

As I lay there, poised, my mind raced. We couldn't run, not with William's wheelchair. We certainly couldn't outrun a bear. We had no escape.

All my senses were on high alert. I listened to my children breathing, fast asleep, unaware of the danger that lurked just outside. My breath was as quiet, slow, deep, and as even as I could make it.

I fervently prayed for protection and safety the entire night. My eyes were pinned to where I knew the line of the horizon should be. I was actively waiting, constantly beseeching the Lord for protection and deliverance. Through it all, I completely trusted God to get us out. I did not think about being scared. I knew God could see us *and the bear*. I knew He was in control, and I could trust Him to rescue us.

At one point in the night, I heard the bear's heavy paws hit the top of the cabin wall and drag down. Later, as the first gray light of dawn began to emerge, I quietly got out of bed. I looked around the open cabin and found a small hatchet someone had left behind. Armed with just a small hatchet and flashlight, I crept down the steps and slowly walked around the perimeter of the cabin.

There was no bear in sight. But underneath our cabin was a huge hole dug out like a giant bowl.

It made me think of Daniel in the lions' den. I believe God made this bear drowsy. The bear must have made a bed underneath us and slept there for the night. When the children awoke, we ate breakfast, packed, and left.

Reflection

As I drove home, I felt God tell me to be ready because something big was going to happen. I needed to be alert, watching, listening, and waiting for what He wanted to show me, like I stayed alert throughout the night because of that bear. I was steadfast and ready, trusting in His timing, not knowing what was going to happen or when.

Life carried on as normal; I was just more focused throughout the day. As I went about my routines, my mind tuned in, ready to respond to God. I maintained an open mind and heart for what God might be prompting in me.

Isaiah 40:31 says, "But those who wait in the Lord will renew their strength. They will soar on wings like eagles; they will run and not grow weary; they will walk and not be faint."

In my experience, this type of waiting is not impatient, bored, or trying to force change. Instead, it's looking to God in expectation, waiting for His signal, for Him to show us His work. This active waiting trains our hearts to listen to the inward voice of the Lord. A. W. Tozier gives us this guidance:

"Retire from the world each day to some private spot. Stay in the secret place 'til the surrounding noises begin to fade out of your heart and a sense of God's presence envelops you. ... Listen for the inward voice 'til you learn to recognize it. ... Learn to pray inwardly every moment. After a while you can do this even while you work. ... Never let your mind remain scattered for very long. Call home your thoughts. ... Practice spiritual concentration of God and men."

I would encourage you to carve out time each day to sit still and listen to the Lord. Give yourself time to let go of thoughts and worries. Breathe slow and deep. Invite God to join you. He already knows your thoughts, cares, and needs. Don't fill this time spewing all that's weighing you down. That will only distract you from His message and make you tense. Ask Him to fill you with His peace, wisdom, and love.

God responds; He gives me words, messages, or encouragement, while I sit with Him in quiet. It takes practice, but as it becomes a regular part of the day, you become more sensitive to His guidance.

God does not want us to live in anxiety or with chaotic thoughts. When we are connected to Him, we gain stability and are able to respond. We gain understanding of situations and consider others' needs before reacting to what we see on the surface.

The camping experience wasn't about the bear. It was about my response and where my focus was. Yes, I had to be alert and ready to do whatever to protect my family. I also knew I was completely powerless. My focus was not on that bear, it was on God.

I like what Corrie ten Boom says about this kind of heads-up from God: "If God shows me bad times ahead, it's enough for me that He knows about them. That's why He sometimes shows us things—to tell us that this too is in His hands. Lord, make us ready to do your will and not our own. Your power is ours when we follow your guidance. What a comfort!"

At that moment, camping with the bear, I didn't have a plan, and I didn't have control. I stayed still, my eyes fixed on where the horizon should be. God prompted me to be ready, to keep intensely focused and alert. A large change was going to happen soon. Five months later, we fled our home.

PART 3

Single Mom

New Beginning

One rainy night in January, my husband was in a fit of rage. He threw a precious item of mine against the wall and then kicked me across the living room floor, in front of the children. In my peripheral vision, I could see my children frozen. To my knowledge, they had never witnessed any of the physical abuse I suffered. I was concerned about what they were seeing and feeling but mostly for their safety. My husband yelled, "You and the kids leave; I don't ever want to see your faces again."

For so long, I had believed it was my responsibility to stay as long as my unbelieving spouse wanted me to. God knew I was waiting for the right words and moment.

1 Corinthians 7:15 says, "But if the unbeliever leaves, let it be so. The brother or the sister is not bound in such circumstances; God has called us to live in peace."

Like a blast of fresh air, I was struck with hope. This was it. My unbelieving spouse told me to leave. It was like a timer went off in my soul. I was done and free to go.

I knew I needed to take advantage of this window of time. Urgently, I gave each kid a black, plastic garbage bag and told them to fill it with whatever they wanted. I didn't care if it was toys, books, or clothes.

Meanwhile, my husband got into my purse. He took what little cash I had and cut up my bank and debit cards. He left the house as we gathered our things.

I quickly filled my bag with personal essentials, grabbed all of my son's medical equipment, and got our cat. We were packed up and in the van in less than a half hour.

As we loaded into the van, my husband came through the front door. While we drove to my mom's house, Kay asked, "Are we ever going back?"

I said, "No."

There was a sigh of relief from everyone.

Not long after, we showed up on my mom's doorstep. I don't remember what I said or her initial reaction. But I do remember we were enveloped by the light and warmth of her home. We had found a safe harbor.

I got the kids settled into beds near their typical bedtimes. They had spent nights there for holidays, so it was not an unfamiliar setting. I stayed positive and encouraged them that things would get better.

After bedtime, my mom heard, for the first time, what our lives had been like for the past ten years. The next morning, my brother came over and was filled in on the night before and the history that we'd been living. Rick and my mom were supportive and practical, looking at next steps, and helping me make a plan. They realized this was not a short-term separation but the beginning of a different life that would affect us all.

We were at the start of a new beginning.

Reflection

In those first few days, I wanted to wallow and reflect. However, I realized that for the kids, I did not have the luxury of dwelling in self-pity. So I jumped into action. I kept the kid's schedule as normal as possible. They stayed in the same school for the remainder of the year. Still in this whirlwind of uncertainty, I knew we were not alone. I knew God saw us and would take care of us. These words came to mind from the timeless hymn:

His Eye Is on the Sparrow
Why should I feel discouraged?
Why should the shadows come?
Why should my heart feel lonely
And long for heaven and home?
When Jesus is my portion
A constant friend is he.
His eye is on the sparrow
And I know he watches over me.

This hymn is based on the verse that says, "Are not five sparrows sold for two cents? Yet not one of them is forgotten before God." Luke 12:6 and Matthew 10:31 also say, "So do not fear; you are more valuable than many sparrows." This scripture reassured me God had not taken His eyes off of us, and He would take care of us, protect us, and provide for us.

Regardless of your situation, even if it seems like God is distant, He has not turned away from you. Trust Him to walk you through the dark and messy paths of life. You are valuable to God, and He is mighty to save.

In the Bible, God gives the message "Do not fear" or "Fear not" many times over, for a reason. Think of it this way: If we see one of our children try their best to solve a problem and then finally turn to us for help, aren't we rejoicing in our hearts? The mighty mama and papa bear warriors are proud of their children for standing their ground, for doing what's right. We are ready to go to bat for them, comforting them, and letting them know everything is going to be alright. That is how Father God is with us and more so because He is love. So we have no reason to fear. Even though a new beginning can feel like stepping off a cliff, God is there to protect us.

A Step at a Time

The day after we fled, my brother encouraged me to call the Department of Human Services (DHS) to see what help might be available.

But it was extremely hard for me to make that call. The receiver felt like it weighed a thousand pounds. I didn't want to be one of *those* people, on public assistance. When they answered the phone, I requested information about food stamps. I could barely complete my question. I was so choked up; ashamed, I started crying. I dreaded the stigma and felt like a failure.

However, the woman on the phone was kind and encouraging. She gently said, "This is only for a season. You are going to be alright." I got into the home to work program, through the Department of Human Services (DHS) and went through a series of workshops.

Instead of feeling shame, it felt good to be able to contribute and provide for my family. The food stamps and the financial support gave me the buffer needed until I was able to secure a job. I appreciate the dignity it gave me to take care of my family and myself while I worked to become more financially stable.

After finishing the workshops, I applied for jobs. I was hired by the local school district as a part-time teacher's assistant. The job was perfect. Even though the pay was little, the hours allowed me to drive my kids to school each day. My kids were also able to stay at their same school with their teachers and friends.

Although I worked to maintain a normal schedule, my kids and

I were walking wounded. Our lives changed in an instant, forever. We missed our neighborhood and friends, the walk to and from school, playing in the park on the way home. The kids' frustrations led to arguing and petty squabbling. With tight living quarters, we had little room for grace, and irritations arose easily. We needed to grieve, but I was also intent on putting our best foot forward.

After three months at my mom's, it was obviously too much for two women to run a house and feel autonomous at the same time. With the help of the housing authority, I was able to look for a home. I wanted a quick turnaround and was willing to do whatever it took.

One afternoon, I expressed my frustrations to my brother.

He said, "It took ten years to dig this hole; it may take ten years to fill it and gain some ground."

Instead of finding that discouraging, it gave me perspective. I just had to keep taking positive steps. There is no quick fix, just persistence. By June the kids and I moved into a place of our own, a townhouse with plenty of room for us all.

Reflection

All along, the Lord led me, step by step. He provided what we needed at each moment, not overwhelming me with too much at once.

My anthem was "Be Thou My Vision," a hymn that talks about the Lord being first in my heart, His presence being my light. God was my light. I listened; He guided me. I sought Him; He was always there. I felt it. I knew it. I read it in His Word.

One summer, I had two dear friends from Florida visit me in the Northwest. While together, we went on a cave adventure, where I experienced the deceit of darkness.

My son guided us as we walked along with headlamps strapped to our helmets. However, deeper into the cave, my lamp went out. If I trained my eye to my son's lamp, I could see the next step, but when he turned his head, I was in complete darkness.

At one point, I stood on the top of a rounded boulder and began to lose my balance. My son's lamp was turned away, but I thought I saw the reflection of light beside me on the damp cave wall. I saw a wall I could lean to for support. I lurched my body to catch the wall but soon discovered there was no wall there. I yelled, "Help me," but was already on my way down.

Getting back up, I had big bruises and had ripped my favorite jeans. Yet, it was a good reminder of what happens if I move forward without light on my path. I put my trust, reaching for support from something that wasn't there.

Sometimes in life, we reach for achievements, security, or people in our darkness, only to find they were not equipped to help us. God wants us to walk in His light; He wants to guide us on His path.

Around the time my family and I were adjusting to me being a single mom, I was given a book written by Stormie O'Martian called *Just Enough Light for the Step I'm On*. In her book, she says, "Sometimes only the step I'm on, or the very next one, ahead, is all that is illuminated for me. ... At those times I walk in surrender to faith, ... because it is God who has given me that light. ... I must ... allow God to get me where I need to go. I walk forward, one step at a time, fully trusting that the light God sheds is absolutely sufficient."

Moving forward on our own, without His light and guidance, is like groping in the dark; we likely will fall, get hurt, or become lost. When we trust God in each step, He lights our way and ensures our step ahead. He wants us to include Him as our light on the journey, so we can walk together through the darkness, a step at a time.

Unclenched Hands

After leaving my husband, life had turned upside down and spun out of control. Beginning a new life with six kids, including a child who was significantly disabled, felt like moving a building. To survive, my focus became very narrow.

We took so little with us when we left that I readily acknowledged all I had belonged to God. With a grateful heart, I held everything with an open hand. Well, everything except my kids.

They were *my* kids, my heart. I loved them more than life itself. I held them so tightly; I did not want to lose them.

When each of my children were babies, I wanted to dedicate them to the Lord, acknowledging this commitment in front of my church family. However, my husband wouldn't allow it. Although he never attended church with us, I honored his wishes.

But now that I was their sole parent, God wanted me to entrust my children to Him, to surrender my kids' lives to Him. I remember a specific time when I blustered with God about this. I said, "No! I'll take care of them. I love them. I don't want to give them to you. No one loves or cares about them more than me. I can't. What if you take them from me?"

As I paused and sat quietly, the Lord spoke to my heart, reminding me that He knows my kids better than I do. He said to me, "I love them more than you and more than you could imagine."

I realized then He was right. He knew the plans He had for their lives. He loved them beyond what I was capable of showing. So slowly, I loosened my grip.

I was reminded of Matthew 7:11, which says, "If you, then, though you are evil, know how to give good gifts to your children, how much more will your Father in heaven give good gifts to those who ask him!" God is sovereign and already knows my children's whole stories. He sees the big picture and knows what is best for them.

Slowly and finally, I opened the clenched hands that held my children so tight. I committed my children to Him. Even though it is not typical to dedicate older kids (my oldest was eleven and youngest five), I asked the church elders if I could publicly dedicate my children to God. To my church family, it may not have seemed a big deal. To me, it was relinquishing the last of what I withheld from the Lord. It was a public statement of a private commitment I had made with Him.

Reflection

I had plans for my family, for each child. I wanted my kids to live enriched by happy memories, family experiences, good education, and biblical truths surrounded by the family of God. I would be the one to provide this for them. Rooted in love, I wanted to keep them wrapped up in my heart. But God's word reminds us of His sovereignty and where our plans fit into it.

Proverbs 16:2 says, "All a person's ways seem pure to them but motives are weighed by the Lord," and James 4:14–15 says, "Why, you do not even know what will happen tomorrow. What is your life? You are a mist that appears for a little while and then vanishes. Instead, you ought to say, 'If it is the Lord's will, we will live and do this or that.'" These verses help me to see I can trust in God, in His timing, process, and goodness.

I held my children so tightly that I created a barrier separating me from God. I had to fully trust Him, give up everything and follow Him completely. It was much easier for me to loosen my grip once I was gently reminded of His great love for my children. They are His children, after all.

I encourage you to ask God, "Is there anything I am withholding from you? Anything I feel would be best in my control? Is there anything You want me to release to Your care?"

Maybe you are like Gollum from *The Lord of the Rings*: crouching and covering what is most precious to you. If so, you are robbing yourself of the blessing of seeing the ways God can work with what you hold most dear.

Be open with the Lord; ask Him to make you aware of anything you are gripping too tightly. Release this to God, so He can help you grow in your relationship with Him.

When the path ahead feels uncertain, when we desire to see or understand the outcomes, let us consider Psalm 138:8, which says, "The Lord will vindicate me; your love, Lord, endures forever—do not abandon the works of your hands." God in His omnipotence cares for you and what concerns you. Choose to trust Him with your journey and those who are on it with you. Hold your life with an open, unclenched hand. Watch and see His loving-kindness accomplish His work for your life, providing for you with His mighty hands.

Stability: God Provides

As soon as I got a job, I made arrangements to repay the student loans my husband allowed to default. I faithfully paid each month, but at tax return time, all of my refunds went straight to student loans. It took about four years, but I was so proud to pay them off.

My husband, who never filed taxes, owed a huge amount to the IRS, including penalties and overdue charges. During the divorce proceedings, he tried to saddle me with half, stating that it was only fair. I argued my case to the judge, explaining I had repeatedly urged my husband to file and adding that none of the W-2s were in my name. Thankfully, the judge did not lay that burden on me.

However, lack of finances brought me anxiety, especially during that first year as a single working mom. I remember lying awake at night, going through everything we owned, trying to think what I could sell. I quickly realized I didn't have anything worth selling.

There were years the income did not match the outflow of needs and bills. If you were to put it down on paper, eyebrows would raise and question marks would appear.

Still, each month God provided. One time at the grocery store checkout, I was short the amount due. I stood there doing the math of what groceries to take out when the lady behind me offered to pay the whole bill. I was astonished and overwhelmed with such gratitude. Every time there was a wedding, funeral, meeting, or training at the church, someone would show up at our door, laden with leftover food.

Unfortunately, our van broke down soon after arriving at my mom's. The repair shop said it would be over three hundred dollars to fix. It might as well have been three thousand. I had no job or means to pay for repairs. I prayed. A week later, I received a check in the mail from someone I didn't know from North Carolina.

Later, I found out my sister told her Bible study about our needs. Someone from her Bible study shared with someone else, and eventually, word spread. A woman in North Carolina held a spaghetti dinner fundraiser for our family. The check happened to be the exact amount needed to repair our van. I was astounded. That is the work of God right there. Experiences such as these helped me to develop the habit of praying to God about our specific needs and wants.

Reflection

It is hard and embarrassing to ask for help. It took time for me to humbly accept financial support. I wasn't ungrateful or rude but kindly would say, "No, thank you," out of shame. Then I was reminded by an elder in my church that I should gratefully receive gifts given to my family, so others may be blessed in their giving. James 1:17 says, "Every good and perfect gift is from above, coming down from the Father of heavenly lights, who does not change like shifting shadows." There is no change in God's character, He has no ulterior motives; He has no strings attached to His gifts and provisions for us. We should accept gifts from God with gratitude. We need to allow others to clear the path ahead when our feet are weary from the journey.

I was also reminded of 2 Corinthians 9:7–8, which says, "Each of you should give what you have decided in your heart to give, not reluctantly or under compulsion, for God loves a cheerful giver. And God is able to bless you abundantly, so that in all things at all times, having all that you need, you will abound in every good work."

A cheerful giver, giving to an ashamed receiver, may inhibit the grace and blessing of receiving. So I learned to lay aside my false pride and unfounded shame, and gratefully receive God's provision and blessings.

I learned with time to look to God as the head of our household. I talked over finances and bills with the Lord, much as a wife discusses budgeting with her husband. After the kids went to bed, I imagined Jesus sitting there at the foot of the bed with me, going over each bill. I laid out each specific amount due and broke it down subtracting each amount from that month's paycheck. Tallying up the total, I told Him that we need a certain amount of money. I always submitted my ideas to Him, for example, I could try to work another job, or I could maybe get a loan. Yet it never failed, He always had a third answer, something I had not even considered.

In the end, we never went without our needs being fulfilled. His resources are limitless. His ways of providing and healing our family were far better than what I could have done on my own. As Isaiah 55:8–9 shares, "'For my thoughts are not your thoughts, neither are your ways my ways,' declares the Lord."

Healing and Redemption

After we left, I went through a tough transition toward healing. Through the season of separation and divorce, the Lord brought me healing and redemption.

Mental Healing

In Christian culture, a harmonious marriage is expected. This can make it extremely difficult to discuss your abuse with a counselor or pastor. It feels like a floodlight of shame bearing down on you. But sharing in a safe environment leads to healing. I needed a very trusted counselor, friend, and pastor to walk me through my past traumatic experiences.

In the first year after we left, I faithfully went to counseling every week. My husband's accusations and verbal threats had wormed their way into me, filling me with guilt. I was in such an insecure place, I regularly second-guessed many of my decisions. I had to write in a journal why I was leaving him so I couldn't be manipulated, and I referred back to it often.

These scriptures gave me mental grounding, in the midst of accusations and name calling. Isaiah 41:10 says, "So do not fear, for I am with you; do not be dismayed, for I am your God. I will strengthen you and help you; I will uphold you with my righteous right hand." Psalm 32:7 shares, "You are my hiding place; you will protect me from trouble and surround me with songs of deliverance."

Spiritual Healing

I turned to my relationship with Christ first when my direction was unclear, when we were in danger, or when I felt uncertain. God demonstrated His faithfulness to me through discernment and creativity every time I asked for it. I learned to keep my antenna up and my mind tuned in so I could focus on His leading.

A year into separation, I got a phone call from my husband. He said he had a dream where I stood before him in a tattered wedding gown, bruised. God spoke to him, saying, "Why have you battered my bride?" God called my husband to account for how he treated me. God stood in front of me. He claimed me as His bride. God spoke directly to me through my husband's retelling of his dream. This reassured and strengthened me. I knew God was standing with me, and I could trust His wisdom.

Divorce

I remained separated from my husband for two years. I asked him to do three things: go to counseling, go to anger management, and get involved in a church. I knew he needed accountability, mentoring, and discipleship. After two years, he made no move towards these steps. My brother encouraged me to speak with the elders. I asked for the pastor's wife to be present too. After I shared, they recommended I proceed with divorce, for our safety. The elders explained my husband had already broken his marriage vows by abusing me. Gratefully, my brother came with me to meet the church elders. When I told them my stories, they were empathetic and supportive. As we were leaving that night, Rick said, "See, you've lost a husband, but you've gained more brothers who are supporting and helping your family."

Before our divorce, we were required to go to mediation. My husband was disagreeable, unwilling to compromise. Because of his disposition and increasing anger, the mediator was unable to mediate. My husband left in a huff.

I stayed in the foyer of the office to give him ample time to leave the building. As I got off the elevator and rounded the corner, there he was, waiting for me. My heart jumped in fear. He badgered and threatened me. I left out of the opposite side of the building and hurried to where I had parked.

Reflection

Healing: Forgiveness

It is a long haul for mental, spiritual, and emotional healing to take place; there is no quick fix. Separation or divorce does not make everything better. You need outside help and trustworthy, faithful friendships to see you through. With the help of a counselor, clergy, close friend, or relative, it may take years to unravel the confusion and damage done from abuse. Give yourself grace.

The first step to healing is forgiveness. You must forgive yourself and seek forgiveness for any part you have done wrong. You may need to ask God to reveal what you need to ask forgiveness for. This way, you can be freed from guilt and the accusations. You will then be able to stand strong in the truth that all is right between you and God.

The next step is a hard one: You must forgive your abuser. Understand, forgiveness does not equal reconciliation. Forgiveness is not erasing the wrong. Forgiveness releases you from the burden of bitterness. It is not your place to exact judgment. God, Who cares for you and protects you, will deal with your abuser in the way He sees fit; let it go. Every time feelings of injustice, anger, sadness, guilt, remorse, or retaliation creep in, turn it over to God. He will take care of it.

Redemption

God can and will redeem years that have been stolen. Isaiah 61:3 points to His restoration. He says He will "provide for those who grieve in Zion; to bestow on them a crown of beauty instead of ashes, the oil of joy instead of mourning, and a garment of praise instead of a spirit of despair. They will be called oaks of righteousness, a planting of the LORD for the display of his splendor."

When our hopes for a happy marriage and family are dashed, we mourn. We become discouraged when we don't see change for the better. However, God renews us. He strengthens us like mighty oak trees, standing tall and strong, depicting His righteousness.

I was in puppy love as a teen. I would see something that reminded me of the boy I was dating and looked forward to telling him about my experiences. He was always foremost in my thoughts. Later, I realized that is how it is with God. I want to point things out to Him and share them with Him. He has become part of my every moment, conversation, and thought, but guess what? He is also thinking about me. Zephaniah 3:17 is one of my favorite verses; it encourages me and brings me life and strength; it says, "The Lord your God is with you, the Mighty Warrior who saves. He will take great delight in you; in his love he will no longer rebuke you, but will rejoice over you with singing." What a great realization. Doesn't that sound like someone who is in love with you?

He is here, near, ready to save and protect, calming anxious thoughts with reassurance of His love. He is the hope that never disappoints. In this difficult season of transitions, God made it very clear and specific: He is my defender and protector; He brings me rest and healing.

It is this healing that provided me with the courage to face the unexpected moments on my journey as a single mom.

Edge of the World

After a fun spring-break weekend at the coast, the kids (ages seven to twelve) and I were headed home in our nine-passenger van. Will, in his wheelchair, was locked down in the way back. Earlier that day, we received word that my nephew and his wife had just had their first baby. I had bought the softest baby blanket for him and had it in a small bag on the floor, between the driver's and front passenger seats.

I decided to take Highway 101 along the Oregon coast for the scenic view.

The view was beautiful. I noticed the late afternoon sun was glistening on the ocean and waves below, causing them to sparkle and shine. The sky was a lovely summer blue, with feathery clouds brushing the edges of the horizon. Our van climbed, then dipped, following the curves of the hillside to our immediate right, weaving to the right and then swaying to the left. On our right, the forested greens of the hills looked enchanted as the sun glinted through, spotlighting areas here and there. On the left, the majestic roar of the ocean, the call of the seagulls, and the salty sea air filled our senses, giving us a complete sensory experience as we enjoyed this wondrous drive.

What I didn't notice was one of the children getting green around the gills. I heard a holler that one of the kids was going to throw up. I wanted to get the car-sick one out before the baby gift we just bought was blasted with the remains of lunch.

With a break in traffic, I yanked up the bag holding my newborn grand-nephew's baby blanket and whipped the van left across the four lanes, towards a small turnout along the coastline. Our wheels met the small stone wall in that turnout. However, instead of stepping on the brake, I hit the gas. Our van lurched over the wall. The front of our van hung over a cliff going straight down to the ocean. We were at least seventy feet up.

Wide-eyed, we froze. The van wavered between asphalt and air. I slowly turned to the kids and said, "Don't. Anyone. Move." In my mind, I could see tomorrow's headlines: "Mother and Six Kids Plunge to Death on the Oregon Coast."

We sat still for several minutes, as we teetered on the edge of the world. I told the kids to slowly exit, one at a time, and stand away from the van. Ryan was the first to step out. The two oldest got Will out of the back in his wheelchair. When everyone was safe, I got my purse and met them against the stone wall.

After some inward deliberation, I decided I could rock the van back onto the asphalt. Leaving the kids at a safe distance, I went back to the van. First in reverse, then back to drive, I punched the gas pedal with my foot. My stout-hearted efforts were to no avail.

Back to the wall, we talked about what we were going to do. We did not have roadside assistance, and I did not have money for a tow truck. We had no cell phone reception. With an indomitable spirit, I reassured them that everything was going to be fine. We prayed. We tried waving down people for help. No one stopped.

It was early evening and getting cool. A man in a small car with a large German shepherd stopped to help. He said his little car couldn't do much to help, but he had a friend over the hill who owned a tow truck. He would let his friend know we needed help. We thanked him, said goodbye, and waited. After it turned dark, a man with a tow truck showed up. We asked him if he knew the man with the big German shepherd. He said they had never met.

Reflection

To this day, the kids are not entirely sure the man with the dog wasn't an angel. Hebrews 1:14 says, "Are not all angels ministering spirits sent to serve those who will inherit salvation?"

The Bible explains angels do a number of different services for God; they deliver messages, accompany the lonely, grant protection, and fight battles. They carry out the assignments given to them by God and typically do not draw attention to themselves. I work to never put God in a box. That way, I remain open and expectant to how He answers requests. Maybe it was an angel who helped us that day. Maybe it was an ordinary man. The one thing I know: It was not an ordinary circumstance. God listened and heard us call for help, and He sent it.

While waving down folks for help, we had hope. We knew that in the end, everything would turn out alright. Besides, we already had much to be thankful for: We were all alive, unharmed, and had not teetered off the edge of the world. We knew in prayer that God would take care of us.

1 John 5:14–15 says, "This is the confidence we have in approaching God: that if we ask anything according to his will, he hears us. And if we know that he hears us—whatever we ask—we know that we have what we asked of him."

I have learned to pray to God in confident expectation. I can approach His throne of grace any time and know He listens. I can rest knowing there is nothing that shocks Him; no situation is beyond His reach. He knows me better than I know myself. He understands my thoughts from afar, and He has a plan for how everything is going to turn out.

I want to encourage you that in our many life circumstances, we are not unseen by God. Even when there is no cell service, or we feel we are alone in the dark, and it seems we are invisible to others, God sees us. He understands our fears and our thoughts. He is never too far to help and always has a plan to start moving forward again. No matter how mucky, muddy, or difficult the situation, even if you are to blame, God mercifully responds to our cries. He provides a way to walk forward. Don't hesitate to ask God for help out of a sticky or even disastrous situation. Don't let shame or pride keep you from calling out to Him. He can be our first and our last thought in good times and in times of trouble. He can be trusted to be faithful.

Becoming Farsighted

I had been a stay-at-home mom for most of my kids' lives. So when we moved to our townhouse, and I started working full-time, there was a lot of adjusting. In order to keep up with the household chores, the kids had to take on new responsibilities.

One important job was getting William off his school bus. Whoever was home needed to wheel him into the garage, unstrap him, and carry him up the stairs to our main floor.

Sometimes, one of the kids would start preparations for dinner. And most of all, I wanted the living room to be straightened up before I got home.

Yet it seemed no matter how many family meetings we had, after work, I came home to the aftermath of a tornado. I immediately would get frustrated and start yelling for things to be picked up.

But then, one day, I stopped to consider, what will their childhood memories be? I didn't want my kids to remember Mom always screaming and demanding. I asked myself, is this going to matter five or ten years from now?

I took a step back and got a glimpse of the big picture. Instead of being disappointed or frustrated about what they hadn't done, I learned to hone in on what their day was like. I was available and open to hear their discouragements and their joys.

Looking back, I see that God was faithful. Answering my consistent prayers, He helped me see past the surface and inspired me to alter my approach.

Reflection

Choosing to become farsighted inspired me to be intentional in real conversations. I focused on developing relationships with my kids through shared thoughts and ideas, camaraderie, laughter, and empathy.

I've found I can easily get caught up in day-to-day routines, unmet expectations, and what should happen. I can become irritated and sidetracked, reacting in a manner that does not factor what will matter next month or next year.

Being farsighted helps me have an eternal perspective and rein in my responses based on reality versus expectations. 2 Corinthians 4:17–18 helps redirect my perspective from what is temporary to what is lasting. It says, "For our light and momentary troubles are achieving for us an eternal glory that far outweighs them all. So, we fix our eyes not on what is seen, but on what is unseen, since what is seen is temporary, but what is unseen is eternal."

I encourage you to become farsighted. This will help you train up your children with a focus on what is unseen and eternal. I am not recommending you minimize the experiences kids have. However, try to help them visualize years past where they are now. Help them see that in the grand scheme of things, their current struggles may be tough but are temporary.

Take a step back, look long into the future, and consider what your words, actions, patterns, and habits are developing in your kids. What do you want their memories to be?

Whatever the answer to that question is, be intentional about cultivating your response so you do not get bound up in daily encumbrances. Do not let the everyday circumstances distract you from the core of what matters: character development and lasting relationships. Parents who become farsighted can better guide their families by investing life-giving affirmation into their kids. Keep your eyes on the horizon; intentionally reflect on the legacy you are building. Focus on the memories your kids are making while walking on the path of life alongside you; they will be cherished for years to come.

Fearless Faith

One early evening in January, I was driving my youngest daughter and my sons home from an orthopedic appointment for Will. On the familiar route home, my eyes scanned the dark road and sidewalks. Passing a corner, I saw a small cluster of people gathered; someone appeared to be naked on the ground. I couldn't tell what was going on but knew something wasn't right. I couldn't keep driving past.

I pulled over and told the kids to stay in the van. After a quick prayer, I locked the doors and headed to the corner. As I walked toward the person crumpled on the sidewalk, two large men came towards me. In my most "in charge Mom" voice, I demanded, "What's going on here?" I pushed between the men and continued marching toward the injured person.

In response, they started to whine, "Well, she—" I didn't wait to hear any more. I was appalled; there was a woman on the ground, half-naked. She had been kicked and beaten. I helped her sit up and regain her composure. I stayed with her until help arrived and told the responding officer I'd be willing to testify in court.

When I got home, I realized what a dangerous situation that could have been. But I was fearless. Because of my faith in God, I knew I was doing the right thing. I felt prompted to stop and responded, knowing I wasn't doing it alone.

The next day, I got a call from the officer; he thanked me for stopping to help. He told me the woman had suffered damaging blows to her ribs and head, and had internal bleeding. If I had not stopped, she would likely have died. Several months later, I received a call from the police, asking me to recount the incident. I told them what I saw and affirmed I would testify. When the men heard I was willing to testify, they confessed and were sentenced without trial.

On another occasion, Will was in the hospital, fighting for his life. He had developed peritonitis (a bacterial infection) from a g-tube placement surgery. He was in a great deal of pain. He had a shunt in his head to drain excess spinal fluid from his brain down into his peritoneal cavity.

"The peritonitis germs love plastic," the neurosurgeon explained. Those germs raced up the shunt tubing into Will's brain and were fighting to overtake his little body. The medical team was using the strongest antibiotic available, but this bacterial infection was resistant to antibiotics. There was nothing left to do but pray.

Although I respect the work of the doctors and nurses, my faith was in the omniscient, omnipotent, and sovereign God. Every time Will was hospitalized, I stayed by his side, singing, consoling, encouraging, and praying with urgent expectation.

A pastor came to visit me while we were in the hospital. He was somber and asked why I wasn't crying. How could I be joyful at such a time as this? I explained the doctors did not have the final say over Will's health or life.

The neurosurgeon told me unless Will's natural immune system kicked in, his health would take a drastic downturn. About thirty minutes after the neurosurgeon talked with me, Will's natural immune system kicked in. His body fought that bacterium like a champ. Within days, he was back home, the pain but a memory.

Reflection

Ever since my teenage years, I've held great admiration for Corrie and Betsy Ten Boom. They maintained faith in the Lord Jesus in the face of the horrors endured in a Nazi concentration camp. They even exemplified kindness, compassion, and forgiveness toward their captors.

While Betsy died in the camp, Corrie went on to travel the globe sharing her love for her Savior. One time, God told her to go to Turkey, she didn't know why; she just went. There were so many unknowns: why was she there, where would she stay, what was she to do there? Everything was resolved for her. God met her there.

Her obedience and trust allowed her to help the people He sent her there to meet.

I am quite sure that even the heroes of faith must have experienced times of fear. What sets them apart is that they did not let fear paralyze them into inaction.

In most cases, these heroes were the least likely to be chosen to lead. However, as they responded in obedience to God's leading and sought Him for deliverance, He equipped them for the mission that lay ahead. As Psalm 138:3 says, "When I called, you answered me; you greatly emboldened me." God gives us what we need to do what He calls us to do.

Fearless faith gives us strength; to stand in the face of potential devastation, to forgive our enemies, to stand for righteousness, to do what seems impossible. Fearless faith however is not reckless. It is not foolish and arrogant; it stems from a response to God: listening to and acting on His promptings.

Jennifer Kennedy Dean shares in her book *He Restores My Soul*, "Every act of obedience to the voice of the living and present Jesus steadies the heart. As a house is built brick upon brick, so a steadfast heart is built obedience upon obedience. With each act of obedience, in big things and small things, God is creating a steadfast heart— firmly fixed in place; immovable; not subject to change."

As we respond to the Word of God and His promptings, He reveals Himself to us. As we experience His faithfulness, our relationship with Him deepens.

We can take heart in reading Romans 8:31, 37–39, which reminds us, "What, then, shall we say in response to these things? If God is for us, who can be against us? No, in all these things we are more than conquerors through him who loved us. For I am convinced that neither death nor life, neither angels nor demons, neither the present nor the future, nor any powers, neither height nor depth, nor anything else in all creation, will be able to separate us from the love of God that is in Christ Jesus our Lord."

What may come as a surprise to us does not surprise God. He

too may be saddened, angry, and pained, as He bears our burdens but He is omniscient and sovereign. He equips us with the strength to trudge on our path forward with fearless faith, as we lean into Him.

If we choose to trust God, the uncertain path before us can twist, rise, or fall, but our focus will be on Jesus instead of the circumstances of our journey. Whether calm or climb, the path of life becomes less fearful.

I would encourage you to focus on the one who is proven faithful over the ages. Twinges of fear may still arise, but God sees you, your circumstances, and has a plan to see you through it.

PART 4

Single Mom with Teen/Adult Kids

Chicken Up

With six busy kids, meals were often on the go. Sometimes it was sandwiches in hand as we raced out the door, and sometimes it was drive-through.

One Sunday, we went straight from church to my nephew's piano recital. Fried chicken sounded so right. So we pulled through KFC, ordered lunch, then stepped on it.

The helper of the day (explained in the book's last section) began to pass out the food: potato salad, biscuits, coleslaw, fries, shared drinks … but wait, no chicken. What? How does a chicken place forget the chicken?

Of course, I was pretty upset. I called the number at the bottom of the receipt. They offered to give me the chicken if I came back. We were almost to the recital. There was no turning back. We ate our lunch of sides then piled out of the van to watch my nephew play piano. However, the sides were less satisfying than the main meat of the meal.

Reflection

We have all heard the saying: The main thing is to keep the main thing, the main thing.

KFC's main thing is the chicken. I mean, it is right there in their name.

In Mark 9, three disciples were with Jesus when he went onto the mountain top, and Jesus's "appearance changed from the inside out, right before their eyes … Elijah, along with Moses, came into view, in deep conversation with Jesus. Peter interrupted, 'Rabbi, this is a great moment! Let's build three memorials,' … just then a light-radiant cloud enveloped them, and from deep in the cloud, a voice: 'This is my Son, marked by my love. Listen to him'" (Mark 9:2–7 The Message).

At the time of the transfiguration, Peter, ever the Gung Ho guy, gets excited and makes plans for Jesus. However, it's like God was saying to Peter: stop and listen, already. In this story, I identify with Peter: I am all ideas and action. In this part of scripture, I am reminded to stop, listen, keep the main thing the main thing. I need to spiritually "beef up" or "chicken up," as the case may be.

There are seasons in our lives where we are constantly on the go; hustling from one thing to the next. These activities are good but consume our time. We go on autopilot, mindlessly running through the motions then on to the next activity.

Like the workers of the chicken place, we can just blow right on through a day without making sure to get the meat we need to sustain us; without stopping to get time with God. Lacking that time to sit and listen, we are not fully nourished; we run on fumes.

Running on fumes makes our inner selves irritable, snappy, judgmental, entitled, and resentful. Why? Because other people cannot meet our spiritual and emotional appetite. God alone can fill us up.

When we are on the go as busy moms, dads, grandparents, and so on, it can take time to quiet our minds, to be still and focus. Here are some things we can practice to get to a quiet place internally and focus:

- drive to pick your kids up in a quiet car
- take time to sit quietly in your car during a game or practice
- sit and be still when the house becomes quiet at the end of the day

In these quiet moments, review the day and ask God to point out

- things for which you need to make an apology,
- insight into someone's behavior or words,
- blind spots in yourself/your behavior or habits that need adjusting, and
- reminders to do, say, or reach out to someone.

I know for me, when I took the time to review the day with the Lord, I gained understanding and insight, especially for my children.

There were many times in the teen years, I reacted to a request, behavior, or sibling disagreement without the whole story. In retrospect, in my time with God, I would gain deeper understanding. The next day, I could address the situation in a more uplifting, appropriate, and understanding manner. It is important to be humble enough to admit when we are wrong and apologize, even if it's the next day.

Parenting is hard work and exhausting. Not one of us is always at the top of our game, but somehow, kids expect us to be, and when we make mistakes, it's amplified. If you and I don't take the time to get spiritual protein, then we are filling up on less sustaining sides. We are driving along life's road on our own strengths, which often leads to regrettable actions and decisions.

Take the time to slow down and listen. Pause and listen, look, take in the big picture on the trail of life. Keep the main thing, the main thing. Make an effort to rest in God and build up your spirit.

Memories Made Here

We did not choose to live in the country; it was God's choice for us.

I was receiving housing assistance, and our townhouse no longer qualified under their guidelines. I didn't know what to do and was not looking forward to another move. So I prayed for the next steps for our family.

A teacher at the school where I worked heard we needed a place. It turned out he owned a farmhouse that was available for rent. It was a godsend, perfect timing. However, it was not move-in ready.

The previous renters had kept geese in the upstairs bedrooms, and there was a huge barrel of liquid mercury in the barn. Still, we were up against a time constraint and willing to do what it took.

Both our families worked tirelessly after school and on weekends for weeks to get the house into a livable condition. It was on about three acres with a two-story barn, a chicken coop, fruit trees, and a field. The kitchen cupboards were metal, and there was no dishwasher. There was only one bathroom to share between the six of us, so we had to work out a system.

Moving to the country was a big adjustment for our family. When we were new to country living, my boys rode a school bus to their middle school. I was at work one morning and got a call from Ryan. He explained the man next door had a cow break free and needed help getting it back. He asked permission for him and Thomas to help the man and then walk to school. I said that would be fine. Over an hour later, I got another call. Ryan and Thomas were beside themselves. Once they helped get the cow back, the farmer shot it. It was slaughtering day.

Still, this country house was a great place to raise teens. There was plenty of room to roam and climb trees. An old easy chair made an escape for peace and quiet in the upper level of the barn. Over time, we built a fire pit, tried our hand at gardening and raised chickens, and eventually, we got our goat: Levi.

We have so many great, strange, and funny memories from our six years living in that farmhouse. From college-age to middle school:

Friday night pizza and movie or game nights and s'mores were the kid's favorites. On Sundays, the kids would have their friends over for soup, sandwiches, or salad in the afternoons. One fall, we did what I called Applepaloosa: we had family friends over for apple cider, cobbler, applesauce doughnuts, and apples with caramel dip and played Apples to Apples.

The property was perfect for night games as well, including hide-and-seek and fugitive. One year during our Christmas party, the kids were playing a game called Fugitive. All of the kids were dropped off at the high school parking lot about a mile away from our home. Their objective was to get back to the house before being caught by the few designated as patrol. The kids split up into smaller groups and started to make their way back to the house. Someone from the neighborhood called the police because they saw a bunch of kids running through dormant fields and hiding behind bushes. The police stopped a small group of high school girls. They were so scared and quickly explained the game to the officer. He let the kids off with a warning. Once back at the house, everyone was laughing and regaling stories of being scared by dogs, falling in a ditch, and of course the encounter with police officers. It was the last time we played that game.

Our Christmas parties were the big event of the year, every year. The kids invited as many friends as they wanted. The party would always include a wild and crazy game such as Bigger and Better or a photo scavenger hunt. One year, each team was given five dollars to use at the dollar store for decorations. They then chose a tree in town to decorate and took a picture with it.

Reflection

Growing up, my mom kept our house as neat as a pin. She dusted every week and vacuumed often; dishes were always done after a meal. For me, staying on top of housework with a houseful of kids and working full time was overwhelming. There was always a mountain of laundry to scale. Each of the kids had chores, but staying on top of that wasn't always possible.

For a long time, I struggled with inviting people over. I didn't have a fancy house or live in an upscale neighborhood. I knew my house was not in perfect order.

However, hospitality is in my nature. I love to entertain and host dinners, games, and parties. I came to realize, gathering together and spending quality time with people was more important. I did not have to try to look perfect to impress anyone.

The great thing about having an open home was that it also meant having an open heart for my kids and their friends. I would make it a point to say yes as often as possible whenever my kids asked to have guests over. This way, my kids were invested and motivated in cleaning up or maintaining the house and their rooms.

Once that doorbell rang and the first guest arrived, any panic to get the house in order was over. When guests arrived, the focus was right where it was meant to be: on people.

This reminds me of Martha and Mary, the friends of Jesus. Isn't it so easy to become like Martha and worry when we have guests visit? You suddenly see dust a mile high on the hutch, unswept floors, unvacuumed carpet, and dishes in the sink, and what is that smell? Our senses go on high alert.

Yet, Jesus says Mary has chosen what is better. Time spent with people, learning and investing in each other is better, is lasting. Even as we frantically clean, cook, bake, and bark orders, we need to remember, we are dealing with souls, both those helping with the preparations and the guests in our home (Luke 10:38–42).

Our home was warmed by the people in it. Joy, laughter, and fun transformed our home from wall to wall, spilling out into our neighborhood.

I had a wooden sign that hung in our living room that simply read "Memories Made Here." That was my intention, whether it was filled with friends, extended family, or just our own immediate family; I wanted the memories we created to be treasured.

Make the most of where you are at with little regard for your circumstances. Don't wait for a new job, or a better home, or the right person. Find joy where you are; create family rituals and traditions, and encourage appreciation of the little things.

I once heard someone say, "If you're not where you're at, you're nowhere." If you are waiting for the right things to fall in place, if you are constantly straining for what lies ahead, then you are missing the chance to make lasting memories right now.

I like to reflect on Psalm 17:22, which says, "A cheerful heart is good medicine but a crushed spirit dries up the bones." If you are living with a crushed spirit, seek help. Your joyless spirit is hurting your family. Rediscover gratitude and joy in your everyday life. Your cheerful heart will radiate out to your family, applying the medicine that brings healing. Set the tone that allows for making the most of what you have, wherever you are on life's path. Splash in the puddles, and make the mucky mess fun. Memories are made here, regardless of where here is.

What Now?

From middle school on, Thomas was surrounded by a posse of girls. I would mention that a certain girl liked him, and he seemed oblivious. He would say, "Mom, they are just friends." I would counteract with, "That is not what they think."

He was so kind, creative, and thoughtful with me, his sisters, and friends. Any time we were out together, I never touched a door handle because he always opened and held the doors. When he started dating, I didn't understand why he was an inattentive boyfriend but shrugged it off. In the spring, he asked me how to break up with his girlfriend at the end of their senior year before he went to Hawaii for college.

At twenty-four, Thomas moved back home. After several months, my daughter and I noticed he became moody and angry at times. When asked about it, he became defensive, making up excuses about being busy with classes and work.

One night in an angry outburst, he declared he was moving out. He went to live with Marion, about ten minutes away. Things calmed down, yet there were questions.

A few months later, Thomas asked a few of his siblings, their spouse, and me to meet for pizza at my house. Each of us silently wondered what he wanted to discuss. That night, he came out to us as being gay.

We were shocked, hurt, and sad. We all sat in my living room and cried together. I became agitated. I questioned his faith and recounted his upbringing. I told him the easy thing to do would be to give in to this way of life and said the world would applaud this. His brother Ryan, a new pastor, strongly suggested that he not make *this* his identity but find and maintain his identity in Christ. He recommended he take a year to earnestly seek God and said he would be happy to meet with him to talk if he wanted. The evening ended with hurt feelings, unresolved questions, and no plan moving forward.

Thomas received pats on the back from the few people he had come out to before us. Our reactions were raw and natural, ones of love and care, of history, memories, and broken dreams of future hopes. But for Thomas, it was also very hurtful.

The next morning, I woke up early. Reality fell hard on me like an anvil. My son is gay. I went to my chair in the dining room with my Bible and journal. I was angry at God. I cried, I yelled, I begged. God had told me that He was the father to the fatherless. I dedicated my family to Him. God was their Father. How could He listen to and watch our son in anguish cry himself to sleep night after night, begging for this to be taken from him, and turn a deaf ear? If I had the power and Thomas had come to me crying for help, I would have done it in an instant. I was mad. I asked God, "Why?" Silence. I repeated my "Why?" three more times.

God's response to me was gentle. He said, "'Why' is not your question." It was the only question I had, the only one I wanted an answer to. Even though I was mad at God, even though I didn't understand, I still knew He was the one to turn to. Months later, God told me my question needs to be, "What now?"

Soon after Thomas came out to us, I was told about a book written by Dr. Brad Harper, a professor at Multnomah University, and Drew, his gay son, called *Space at the Table*. I read the book twice. I called the university and asked for an appointment with the author. I was conflicted with my understanding of scripture and how I, as a Christian mom, was supposed to respond. How was I supposed to accept this? Was this my fault?

In *Space at the Table*, Drew Harper writes of Christian parents, "When they ask the question of 'why' does it actually arise from a genuine curiosity or is it from a desire to 'root out the cause' and 'fix' their son or daughter into someone 'normal.' The answer is probably a little of both but from the child's perspective it feels like an attack. The question puts them in a corner and the experience is frustrating and hurtful."

From a divorced mom's perspective, my question "Why?" made me confront whether this was my doing. Did I mother him too much? Did I not provide enough manly influence and opportunities for him growing up? I wanted to race through the past and unravel what went wrong. I did not realize my questions could be hurtful.

Fortunately, Dr. Harper reassured me there was nothing I could have done to ensure a heterosexual Thomas. He said it did no good rehashing Thomas's growing-up years. I couldn't change Thomas; it was not my place. He encouraged me to trust God's plan, to let this be part of his story. He gave me "permission" to go on loving my son as ever before, to welcome Thomas's friends into my home, and even attend his gay wedding, if it ever came to it. Dr. Harper said

Thomas knows my beliefs, he knows where I stand, but he still needs his mom to love and welcome him, not cast him aside.

A week after my meeting with Dr. Harper, I asked Thomas if we could meet for dinner. After we sat, I apologized to him for my initial reaction. I said I was not praying that he would change; instead, I was praying for his protection. During dinner, Thomas read his story to me about living a lie. We cried together.

As Dr. Harper says in the book, "I believe with all my heart that through relationship we can both retain our own views of the world and still come to a place of common ground, of love."

Thomas told me his biggest fear in coming out was losing me. I told him that no matter what happens, he won't lose me.

As I write this, it's been a little over a year since Thomas came out. We've fought and had misunderstandings and hard feelings. But our relationship has remained strong and open.

Reflection

I believe Thomas continues to cautiously hold to a tender faith and belief in God. I told him God may use him to reach a community others would not be able to reach. I trust God is at work in his heart and life. I continue to pray for Thomas to be sensitive to the prompting of the Holy Spirit. I have to let go, for if I try to hold everything myself, I end up getting tangled in things I was never meant to.

I am still working on the "What now?" and my place as a mother of adults and not the fixer. Romans 12:18 says, "If it is possible, as far as it depends on you, live at peace with everyone." This verse has helped me look at my relationship with my son through the filter of peace and faith, allowing his story to be between him and God.

I've learned to trust in God's plan, His goodness, even when I don't understand the process, the reasons, or what the outcome will be. I like the way Pamela Reeve puts it, in her book *Faith Is*. She states, "Faith is … the handle by which I take God's promises and apply them to my particular problems."

In Psalm 9:9–10, God promises He will never forsake those who seek Him: "God's a safe-house for the battered, a sanctuary during bad times. The moment you arrive, you relax; you're never sorry you knocked" (The Message).

Isn't that a wonderful picture? When I can't make the hurt better, when there is nothing I can do to change a situation, I can lay the burden down. I can leave it in God's hands, knowing He's got this, and I don't have to handle it. I can calmly ask, "What now?"

I would encourage you, parents, to live out the message, "The door to our home is always open." Whether that means the physical door or the door to relationship, we need to model unconditional love, even if our kids are not living the life we had hoped. If they are adults, then they are making their own choices. They are on their own life path and journey now. It is their story, and God can intervene any way He wants. Our grown kids need to know there is always an open heart and welcoming arms awaiting them, without any caveats or conditions. Unless they specifically ask for guidance, it is no longer our place. It is our place to love them on their journey and to keep our concerns and hopes between us and God.

Thomas's Story

Below is the letter Thomas shared with me two weeks after he came out to our family as gay. Thomas and I believe it is important to provide his personal insight on this. These are his words, and they are shared with his permission.

Have you ever told a lie that you had to maintain? You know how it goes: One lie turns into two, then four, then twelve. Eventually, you have invented a new reality you have to believe to keep up with your story.

Imagine keeping an elaborate ruse for years. Twelve, to be exact.

I grew up in a Christian church. I professed my belief in Jesus at the young age of six. I read my Bible, went to church, attended Christian summer camp, and went on missions trips.

A bomb dropped in my life shortly after I was baptized. I realized that I was attracted to people of the same sex. Being a strong believer in God and the Bible, I was devastated. I had heard sermons on homosexuality and God's view on it. I started to view myself as an "abomination," dirty and unfit to be a part of God's family.

I thought maybe I didn't believe hard enough. Maybe I wasn't sincere in that salvation prayer. So, I prayed every night to try and secure the grace of God. Anytime there was an invitation: in a sermon, youth group, or summer camp, I prayed along just to be safe. I told myself as long as I prayed about it, and I left it alone, it would go away, and I could be a true, heterosexual Christian.

This was the first lie that I told myself.

I started to pull away from my family and friends, just in case they got close enough to see what I was fighting against. I didn't want to be looked at or treated any differently. I became a very irritable and angry teenager. My family chalked it up to hormones and angst, which was only half-true. For as long as I could remember, I knew I wanted to be married and have kids. How could I be attracted to men as a Christian and still want to have a family? It didn't add up.

I heard that growing up without a dad was "known" to cause boys to be gay. This is because they never got the love and affirmation needed from a male figure. I decided I just needed to heal my childhood, and I would be fixed.

I joined a men's morning group at my church. During this study, we had a chapter focused on "father wounds." I followed every step perfectly. I worked through the pain not having a father had left me with. I came to a point where I truly forgave my father.

The final step was to communicate forgiveness with your father. So, one day while he was over, I told him about his absence and what it had left me to work through. I told him that going through it made me a stronger person and that I forgave him. Before I could finish, he started a slew of curses and told me to go to hell. He sped off, and that's the last I ever talked to him. I had dealt with my childhood trauma. I had healed from it, but I was still attracted to people of the same sex. How could this be? I had "fixed" the root of my problem, right? Wrong.

I created an impenetrable wall around my heart. No one could get in and see my struggle, but I also couldn't get out. My greatest fear was (and is still) being alone for the rest of my life. I am afraid of people abandoning me once they learn the truth about my sexuality.

Being gay in itself (in the church that I grew up in) is not a sin, unless you act on any of those feelings. My mother, two of my sisters, and my brother all went to the same Christian university, majoring in Bible. They also hold this belief. Lying to everyone about one part of me didn't seem like such a big deal. I was lying to myself as well.

However, not accepting myself messed with my ability to trust people to accept me. It also interfered with my ability to trust my thoughts and emotions. I told myself that they loved the "straight me," that I would lose everything when I finally told the truth.

I believed that being gay wasn't an option, and I would recite that to myself over and over again. I cried and yelled at God and begged Him to take it away from me so that I could love and serve Him. I escaped my war zone by hiking or camping.

I sought counseling from a pastor. It was all going well until he told me that I would be cured of my "sinful desires" if my faith was strong enough. I had believed in God since I was six. I watched Him take care of my family when it was impossible. I watched Him save our lives and give all of us the strength to push through all of the hardships we faced. How could I have believed any stronger or had faith that was deeper? The next session, I told him that I was cured so I didn't have to see him or waste any more money.

I listened to podcasts and sermons, and bought prayer journals, devotionals, and Bible study books. I was determined to deepen and strengthen my faith so I would finally be done with the self-loathing. Three years went by. I was closer to God than I had ever felt. I was joyfully serving the church and others outside of the church. I had been described as the funny, loud, and outgoing one. But this all started as an act to keep people away from knowing my hurt. It finally became a natural part of my personality.

The night before my twenty-fourth birthday, everything had become too much, and I broke. I was reading a book that had a very conservative viewpoint on gay Christians. According to this book, I was required to be single and celibate for my entire life. This hit me really hard. I turned to a bottle of tequila. Two shots turned into eight, and I was down and out. Not only was I depressed, but I was also grossly ashamed of myself for getting so drunk. On top of being hung over, I was spiritually and emotionally crushed. I had lost all hope for my life and any kind of reprieve for my pain.

I know from that drunken night that I could not survive a life of celibacy and being alone. Just the thought of being alone for my entire life was unbearable to consider.

I had spent my entire conscious life believing in God. How could I believe in a higher power that created me to have such a strong and instinctual desire for a family of my own when I was also born gay? What loving heavenly Father would torment me for my entire life just to see if I would stay faithful to what He said was right? That wasn't a God that I could follow. Now what? Where do I go from here?

The first step was to finally confess that I had lied to myself. I am gay, and nothing can change that. It took me weeks to bring myself to say it out loud. I still believed in God, but I was confused about how those two parts of my life could fit together. The fear of being condemned to hell for eternity loomed in the back of my mind. Was I gay because I was destined to not be in heaven? These questions unraveled my faith entirely overnight.

I finally decided that I was going to break this cycle. I was going to let someone see the walls that I had built around my heart. It all came out of my mouth in the most awkward and jumbled-up way, even though I had practiced a hundred times. My friend was virtually not affected. She apologized for not knowing and for letting me struggle alone. She offered encouragement and support whenever I needed it and asked how she could help me.

It was the most freeing thing I had ever experienced. We finished dinner like nothing happened, and I drove home feeling like a huge burden had been lifted. After this, I came out to a very select group of people. Every one of them was loving, caring, empowering, and almost anti-climactic, in a good way. No one disowned me. No one accused me of heresy. No one told me I was going to hell.

I finally decided to tell my best friend, who went to the same church as me. She wasn't surprised. She told me that nothing would change in our friendship. We talked about both of our doubts in God, and we were able to engage on a deeper level without my fortress up.

The fear of losing the respect, friendship, and love of all of these relationships is crippling. The possibility of rejection and disownment from the church and my family is something that I can't even begin to describe. It has been a long, exhausting, lonely, and terrifying road, but I know that I am only at the trailhead. I have much, much further to go, many more doubts to conquer. There's a lot of work ahead on the journey to finding happiness, but I know that I am not alone anymore, and that is what keeps me going.

Crying Is for Babies

Ugh, please don't, God; not now. I hate to cry. Let's sort through all of this later. Crying is for babies.

I was at a women's retreat, feeling pretty all together. I'd been having regular God talks, quiet time, and so on. I was there to enjoy girl time.

During one of the sessions, the speaker challenged us: "Is there any lie that the enemy has planted in your mind that you are buying into?" I could not think of any; I mean, I felt solid in my faith and trust in the Lord. I thought I might as well go through the exercise and confirm. So dutifully, silently, while she was speaking, I asked. A tiny little message started dancing around my heart, constricting my throat and bringing tears to my eyes.

Ugh, please don't, God; not now. I hate to cry. Let's sort through all of this later. Crying is for babies.

"For babies?" He prompted. "*I* cried," He gently stated.

I remembered the verse: "Jesus wept" (John 11:35). He did not sniffle and dab his eyes. He wept.

I held it together until I had some time alone. There, leaning against the base of a tree, facing the ocean, I wept, I sobbed, to the point of almost hyperventilating.

I am a failure. I failed in staying pure as a teen. I failed at my marriage, and most painful, I failed at caring for my disabled son, Will.

William, my first son, was born three months early, weighing about two pounds. He was in the neonatal intensive care unit for three months before we could bring him home. He was born with cerebral palsy; he was a quadriplegic, fed through a g-tube, and nonverbal.

Yet Will enriched our lives in very personal and individual ways. We experienced joy in the midst of uncertainty, hardship, and pain. Our hope, faith, and compassion expanded because of our relationships with Will.

A month before Will's fourteenth birthday, the kids and I went to a country fair at a summer camp, where my two oldest were volunteering. It was a fun-filled day, complete with pie contests, three-legged and potato sack races, and more. Will laughed and smiled most of the day. We left late that evening, said goodbye to my oldest daughters, and got home after midnight.

It was hot in the third-story bedrooms, and I was tired. Will's bed was set up in my room so I would be near throughout the night. The box fan in my window, at the head of my bed, was on full blast to alleviate the stifling heat. I fell asleep nearly as soon as my head hit the pillow and slept soundly all night.

The next morning, I got up and found Will had passed away in the night. Cheri slept with me that night and awoke to me discovering poor Will. I was in shock. Frantic! I did not know what to do.

I called my brother. He called the necessary authorities and then came to our house. In the meantime, I wrapped Will in a quilt, while Tabitha woke her younger brothers and broke the news.

We all met downstairs in the living room. When the police arrived, I sat on our love seat, rocking Will back and forth in my arms, saying, "It's all my fault; it's all my fault." I really was half out of my mind with shock and grief. I kept thinking, *If only we had not gotten back so late, I would not have been so tired. If only I had not had the box fan on, I would have heard him. When he needed me most, I was not there. I failed.*

I began asking God, *Why? Why? Did you take him because I was not a good enough mother?* During that past year, I was working full time, going to school full time, along with the constant job of being a single mom to all six kids. It was a lot.

As I sat sobbing at the base of that tree, I repeated in my mind, *I failed. I failed you, God. I failed Will. I was not good enough. That is why You took him from me.* I had stuffed this down and locked it away for ten years because the pain, the wound was too deep. I could not look at it. I could not fix it. I was afraid if I started crying, I would not stop.

Just then, as if over my left shoulder, I heard His gentle voice say, "That is the enemy's lie." At that, I sucked in one last sob and stopped. I asked, *Really? That is a lie?* We sat there together in silence for a while. I breathed. God soothed my heartache.

He said, "We are going to have to reopen that wound and clean it out; it has become infected."

"I hate pain," I said. But I knew if left untreated, it would only fester and become a barrier. This lie would always be a source of unspeakable pain and keep me from complete health. I knew I needed to be free of the lie that I had failed my son.

Reflection

William depended on me (or someone else) for all his needs. Every step of the way, all his life. One of the thoughts that plagued me about the night he died was when Will needed me the most, I was not there for him. It appeared evident this was not a peaceful passing. His bedding was twisted, his body contorted. My feelings of guilt were compounded with questions: *Why did this happen? Why didn't I hear him? It was that box fan. Why wasn't I there to rescue him? Why and how could I sleep through the death of my child?* I slept outside for three nights after Will died. I was beside myself with grief and confusion; outside, somehow, I was closer to him.

God knew the hidden things in my heart and was ready to reveal them to me, to heal me. Daniel 2:22 states, "He reveals deep and hidden things; he knows what lies in darkness, and light dwells with him." I had such pain, guilt, and condemnation hidden so deep in my heart, in my mind. I silently acknowledged the lie: *Yeah, you're right. I failed. God took Will from me because I wasn't good enough. It's all my fault, and now, there's nothing I can do.*

But the Lord crushed those lies. He reminded me of Psalm 139:16: "Your eyes saw my unformed body; all the days ordained for me were in your book before one of them came to be." Will's birth, life, and death were all known by Him before anything took place. Will's entire life was part of God's plan. He assured me that had He wanted me up and by Will's side that night, He could have woken me, as He had done many times since, for other reasons. I still don't understand why He didn't wake me, but I trust God's sovereignty.

Since that day, the scar of that wound remains, but the wound is cleansed and healed. The accusation that I was not a good enough mom rolls off me now like rain off my old red galoshes.

It is a hard thing to address our pain, our wounds, but it is empowering and healing when we do. Are there any lies that have been planted in your mind, in your heart, that you are buying into? Ask God to reveal them to you. Allow yourself to be cleansed and healed, set free from the pain of guilt. Let it go, and let the lies roll off you, never to return.

Powerless

I am a natural fixer. In the face of fear, I am a fighter. For instance, one drizzly day, my kids had cabin fever. So despite the damp weather, they were playing on our back deck, riding their bikes, climbing the tree, when suddenly, I noticed a rat at the edge of the deck. Quickly, I called my kids inside. I went out and threw a bike at it. It sat there and looked straight at me. The nerve. I threw a Big Wheel, then another bike; still it sat there, looking at me.

Well, it was not safe for my kids to play in the back yard with a wild rat on the loose. The rat advanced and was in the middle of the deck now. I looked around the deck; there was nothing left to throw but a Ken doll. Obviously, I had poor aim because I had missed him with every other item I threw. So like a crazy woman, I walked over, Ken in hand, and beat the living daylights (literally) out of that rat (and Ken, for that matter).

When you are the type of person to fight, to fix, to help, it is paralyzing to come up against a situation totally out of your control. When you are completely left out of the decision-making process, it has a life-changing impact. Powerless.

There are specific incidents in my life that took my breath away. I'm not talking about awe-inspiring moments. I am talking about gut-wrenching moments that suck the life out of you. These moments are out of our control. We can't take them back; there is no do-over.

The first was the unexpected death of my firstborn son. After Will passed, I experienced unspeakable anguish. I could not breathe. Losing a child is crushing, debilitating. All parents would give their own lives to spare the pain, suffering, and loss of their children. There is such abruptness to this type of loss. The question why? longs to be answered, and we are left stunned. Powerless.

The second was the complete break in the relationship with my daughter. My heart longed to make things right, to explain, to right misunderstandings on both sides. I longed to share grace, love, and mercy with her. I wanted to fix it. I missed sharing life together, hearing about her days, laughing at her antidotes and experiences, discussing the needs of the world. Any attempt to contact her drove her further away. There was nothing I could do. Losing a child in this way is so personal and perplexing. I was bewildered. Powerless.

Third was when Thomas announced to the family that he is gay. This son of mine, who loves the Lord, served on mission trips, and volunteered at camp, had secretly been struggling with something far beyond my comprehension. I cried for days until I'd used up all my tears. I could not fix this. I could not change it or make it right. I hurt for the private pain, shame, and confusion that he bore alone for so many years. I hurt for what lies ahead for him as he makes choices, as he goes public, and what he may suffer as he moves forward. Powerless.

Reflection

Powerless, except for prayer. Prayer has no boundaries. Prayer is power-full. Even if you can't talk to someone, change a situation, or fix a problem, no one can stop you from using the most powerful weapon at your disposal: prayer. Ephesians 6:12 says that "our struggle is not against flesh and blood but against the rulers, against the authorities, against the powers of this dark world and against the spiritual forces of evil in the heavenly realms."

When we keep our struggles to ourselves, we walk away defeated and resigned. We try to put on a good front, while wrestling against thoughts, temptations, or actions we are ashamed to share. We become exhausted from fighting when we don't enlist others to fight along with us.

Our soul's enemy likes to keep us lost in shame. He likes to make us think we are the only ones who have ever thought or acted like us or experienced what we are going through, isolating and condemning us. However, as we open up, light comes into the darkest parts. We realize we are not alone; there is love, support, and help surrounding us.

This is why we are encouraged to bear one another's burdens, so we can restore the spirit of those who are faltering, in gentleness, not in condemnation and judgment. Galatians 6:1–2 says, "Brothers and sisters, if someone is caught in a sin, you who live by the Spirit should restore that person gently. But watch yourselves, or you also may be tempted. Carry each other's burdens, and in this way, you will fulfill the law of Christ."

And what is the law of Christ? To love your neighbor as yourself. Listen, we are not perfect. As we go through each day, we sin without a second thought. As we bear one another's burdens, we pray together, we are vulnerable, transparent, and love one another. As long as we are doing this, it is difficult to become isolated in shame. Ecclesiastes 4:12 reminds us that a cord of three strands is not easily broken. And Jesus says where two or more are gathered, He is there in the midst of them (Matthew 18:20).

In each of the stories above, I had to rest in God's sovereignty. I had to acknowledge that He knows my children's entire story, and He is good, even when I don't understand. He did not gasp in surprise as each of these painful events unfolded. He already knew. He shared my pain. He loves my children more than I can comprehend. God is weaving their story, and their life choices are between them and God. A Ken doll could do me no good in these situations. The only way forward was into the heavenly Father's arms, allowing my faith to carry me through.

The Lord and I have slushed together through some difficult paths. I rest in the truth that I don't have to solve this, to fix it (whatever "it" is) alone. Neither do you. Handing problems over to the Lord frees us from judgment, frees us to love. We belong to the one who overcomes the muck and mire of the path we are on.

Our Ashes

A fire ripped through our beautiful river gorge. Everyone was struck with shock, fear, and sadness. Many lamented, "It will never be the same."

I recalled countless family adventures there: picnics, hikes, and camping. I remember squeals and screams as we waded through ice cold streams. I reminisced about putting coins on the railroad track, feeling the cooling mist of the waterfalls as we hiked and swam. We never tired of the view each fall on our way to pick apples and pumpkins. We loved taking in the scenery to and from summer camp. It would never be the same.

Many throughout the gorge evacuated. The fire was close enough to our home that I loaded essentials in my car. We prayed as we braced for evacuation. When morning came, the fire stopped creeping our direction.

It will never be the same, I thought, as I stood in front of the mirror the next morning, getting ready for work. But then I thought, *It will heal.*

It will take years. Evidence of the fire will likely be there for decades to come, but beauty will be restored.

As these words came to mind, I reflected on the devastation of my marriage. It was forever changed in a moment. It would never be the same.

We lived in a quiet neighborhood in the heart of southeast Portland. That address holds memories of trick-or-treating, Christmases, playing in the backyard, kittens born under my daughter's bed, popsicles with friends on the front porch. When we left, all the memories we shared there became just that: memories.

It took years, but new experiences arose, new memories were made.

After we left my husband, we made the Columbia River Gorge our playground. We found healing and beauty through the memories we built there.

Our ashes have been turned to beauty. Isaiah 61:3 says, "[He has been sent] to comfort all who mourn, and provide for those who grieve [in Zion] to bestow on them a crown of beauty instead of ashes, the oil of joy instead of mourning, and a garment of praise instead of a spirit of despair."

Reflection

One thing we can be certain of is change. Throughout our lives, there are changes we expect as well as changes that surprise us.

We can take comfort in these verses from Lamentations 3:22–24 (The Message): "God's loyal love couldn't have run out, His merciful love couldn't have dried up. They're created new every morning. How great is your faithfulness! I'm sticking with God (I say it over and over). He's all I've got left."

We can be encouraged by the words of Isaiah 43:19: "See I am doing a new thing! Now it springs up; do you not perceive it? I am making a way in the wilderness and streams in the wasteland." And by Revelation 21:5: "He who is seated on the throne said, 'I am making everything new!' Then He said, 'write this down, for these words are trustworthy and true.'"

There are times in our lives when it seems like we are standing in the midst of rubble; when all we have spent energy building comes unexpectedly crashing down. Throwing out scripture verses feels heartless and trite as we stare at the ashes of our lives.

But as parents, we do not have the luxury of wallowing in our disappointment or heartbreak. We have kids depending on us to set our face like flint and make a new plan.

I am not recommending we ignore a wounded heart or stuff down feelings of anger, fear, and grief. However, we need to model ways of processing these feelings. I strongly encourage parents to seek professional counseling during tough times of change, unexpected loss, and any time when life throws a curveball your way. It is also important to seek professional counseling for your kids, even family counseling.

Please don't ignore the wounds or the scars that disappointment, despair, and heartbreak bring. Just like a physical wound, this needs attention, professional help with mending and healing, salve and binding. This type of help should be open-ended, not a one-shot deal, as reflections and pain may crop up later in life as well.

Be sure to be open with your kids; it is never too late to talk about old wounds and scars, and seek help for them. The good news is, the Lord does make all things new. He wants to heal and bless you. Only He can make beauty out of our ashes.

PART 5

Advice and Reflection

— ❈ —

Making the Most

As a single mom of six kids, I needed divine intervention on a regular basis. Hardly a day went by when I did not pray for wisdom, insight, discernment, and creativity. So in this chapter, I want to share what God taught me to be effective parental strategies for my family. I hope these insights will benefit your family as well.

Household Management

Helper of the Day

On a daily rotating basis, each of the kids had a turn at being the helper of the day. The helper of the day was by my side (when not at school), making dinner, doing laundry, sweeping, and doing dishes. As the helper of the day learned household skills, I heard about their thoughts, feelings, and dreams. Helper of the day got one-on-one Mom time while running errands and riding shotgun if the whole family was going somewhere. This system helped keep the peace, preventing arguments over privileges, because the children knew they would have a turn soon. They knew they could make choices about meals or sides, eating inside or outside, games we played, or movies we watched. I let my children know everything would not be even, but they would have special experiences and outings. For example, if my brother called saying he was going fishing, I could easily say the helper of the day can choose a sibling, and they both could go.

Friday Surprise

Friday was pizza and movie night. The type of pizza depended on finances: from frozen, to make-your-own English muffin or French bread, to a pizza delivery place. After pizza, the kids could choose their Friday surprise. Throughout the week, my kids earned Mom Money by going above and beyond expectations, such as being kind, helpful, and so on. Mom Money could be charged back for being unkind or not following daily expectations. Mom Money could buy bubbles, chalk, super balls, candy, toy cars, coloring books, and other special treats. I also put special time with Mom on the table, such as going on a walk together or getting an ice cream cone: simple, inexpensive, but valuable time together. Coveted special time with Mom was the highest priced item and the one most often saved for. This incentive plan cut down on squabbling; they would often encourage one another instead of arguing, to earn Mom Money for their Friday Surprise.

Family Meetings

We often had family meetings on Saturday mornings. Sometimes, we met to resolve a conflict and make plans for how to handle the situation better next time. We talked about chores and made a list of what needed to be accomplished that day; the kids signed up for the chore they wanted to do. This meant no grumbling or complaining about the tasks because they chose them. We also used this time to plan how we wanted to spend our day or future holidays or birthdays.

Chores

In each room, I taped a list inside a cupboard door of what needed to be done in order for each room to be considered clean. This gave each child a check-off list to go through. When they were finished, they told me to see if everything was done.

Cleaning a bedroom is an overwhelming chore for younger kids. I gave smaller assignments such as putting away all the shoes; when they were done, I gave them another chore. Sometimes, I would sit on the edge of their beds and watch. My sons complained that I would just point and tell them what to do. However, this taught them how to break large tasks into manageable ones until the job was done.

Traditions

Halloween

Costumes were always homemade; we had to be creative and resourceful. One year, the kids all went as a lunch: One was a sandwich, and the others were grapes, a cookie, and a milk box. One year, my youngest couldn't decide if he wanted to be a cow or a policeman, so we settled on a "helper cow": a cow with a badge and a vest that would assist the officers. One year, my oldest dressed as an IRS agent, in a suit with a briefcase and a badge that indicated she was from the IRS.

On Halloween, we drove to my brother's house for hot soup or chili and bread. We'd all eat and laugh, and the cousins would sort, swap, and trade candy.

Thanksgiving and Preparing for Christmas

In November, I had each of the kids write twenty-five "Thankful" notes for friends, teachers, relatives, or each other. The notes simply said, "I'm thankful for you because _____." They handed out these notes or mailed one each day in December, up to the 25th. It was a good way to focus their attention on others, being specific in their compliments.

Instead of the kids trying to buy or make presents for each sibling, we drew names. This way, each kid had one sibling to buy for and one present to receive from a sibling.

Christmas

Christmas was celebrated the whole month of December. In November, we had a family meeting to plan so everyone's favorite activity was included. I got out a calendar, and we would schedule each activity to be sure nothing was missed. My kids said Christmas would not seem complete without

- driving around to look at Christmas lights,
- baking and decorating Christmas cookies,
- watching Christmas movies (each one had a favorite),
- decorating the house inside and out, including the tree,
- going to craft bazaars to shop and get ideas,
- going to downtown Portland to look at all the holiday window displays,
- giving to people in need, and
- hosting our annual Christmas party.

Christmas Party

The Christmas party became something my kids and their friends looked forward to each year. My kids invited as many friends as they wanted and asked each friend to bring a snack to share; this way, we didn't have to worry about having enough food. We made it fun with white elephant gift exchanges and outrageous games like Minute to Win It and relay games.

Fun on a Budget

We didn't have extra money to go on vacation or to the movies or theme parks. However, we lived in the beautiful Pacific Northwest, which allowed us to take day trips to the mountains, forests, high desert, or beach for picnics, exploring, and hiking. Being a tourist in your own area means there are always new places to see and explore.

I kept an ear to the ground for free or reduced-priced activities. Many local attractions had free or reduced-price days: the zoo, art museum, historical museum, children's and science museums. There were opportunities in the summers to go to free concerts and movies in the park as well.

On very hot summer days, we would find a river or lake to splash in. It was just as much fun to take the light rail or city bus into the city and run through the fountains to cool off.

Parades

In Portland, there are two major parades, each a week apart. The Starlight Parade was at night, which means every band, float, and horse is lit up with lights or glow sticks. I loaded our wagon with blankets, snacks, and drinks. At the discount store, I got the kids glow sticks to join in the light-up fun. The next Saturday was the Rose Festival Parade, where every float, horse, and cart was decorated with real foliage and flowers. I picked up sidewalk chalk and bubbles for the kids to play with while we waited for the parade.

State Fair

Going to the state fair was one of our favorite summer traditions. Our state fair had a day you could get in for a canned food donation. We took advantage of that day and were able to enjoy the fair. I knew my kids would be hungry while there, and the smells of the wonderful fair food would be so enticing. So I made the family's favorite: teriyaki chicken and sticky white rice. At lunch time, we went back to the car and ate our meal. I also knew special fair food treats were hard to resist. So I went to Walmart and got giant bagged popped corn and cotton candy to share that we could carry around and snack on as we enjoyed the fair.

Letting Kids Get Involved with Budget

It is difficult for kids to understand the limits of money and to appreciate what they do have. When they were in late elementary and middle school, I had the kids pair up and plan meals, menus, and food with our budget: $200 a month. That was a stretch. It took a great deal of planning, and I only got involved if they had questions. Once the pair had their menu, meal plan, and shopping list, we went to the grocery outlet to stretch our dollars. I silently walked behind them and listened as they discussed buying an off brand to get a better deal and compared prices. Sometimes, they changed their menu to fit into the budget.

Doing this meant little to no complaining about meals. The children all knew they would soon plan meals and work with the budget. They learned to find the best deals and think long term, considering others' wants and needs.

Creative Mealtimes

There were times I spread a blanket on the living room floor and brought in a picnic basket of food: sandwiches and chips with pop or fried chicken with sides. It made a run-of-the-mill dinner an event.

I was also part of a gleaning community. For a small fee, I was able to shop for food from a warehouse that collected donated and discarded items from grocery stores and food businesses. You could usually take as many "mystery" cans (those that no longer had labels) as you wanted. So at least once per month, we would have a mystery dinner. Each of the kids would pick a mystery can, and I would prepare our dinner out of whatever they chose. Sometimes we hit the jackpot; sometimes it was gross. We had drop biscuits with almost every dinner; that would fill tummies if the meal was not desirable.

What I made was what was for dinner, period. However, I did not force my kids to eat something they couldn't choke down. They were welcome to make themselves a peanut butter and jelly sandwich, if they didn't like something we were having.

I got into the habit of packing food and snacks along wherever we went. We brought our own meals to the zoo, city, mall, practically everywhere. We would share drinks and on special outings shakes or pop; in went two straws into three drinks, and we would all still get a treat.

Spontaneity

One Sunday, we were heading home after church, but I felt a heaviness in the ranks. I prayed for an idea. I drove to Winco and got a long sub sandwich, a can of Pringles, and quarter pops from the machines on the way out. Then I drove our van to the back side of the airport. We spread a picnic out on the top of our van and watched planes take off. We imagined where the planes were headed and talked about where we'd like to fly.

Another night, as we were leaving a Boy Scouts banquet, it began to snow. On a whim, I drove up to Mount Hood. At first, the kids were confused. When they realized what I was doing, they were so excited and thankful. I pulled onto a logging road and let them play in the snow.

Once, there was news of a meteor shower. We went to bed early. Then at 1:00 a.m., I woke everyone up, and we headed out to the gorge in our jammies. When we reached our destination, the kids went to the top of the van and looked up at the sky. We brought special snacks and thermoses of hot chocolate. Snuggled in blankets and sleeping bags, we enjoyed fireworks, God style.

Single-Mom Friendship

Soon after we left my husband, I got connected with three other single moms at church. We met on Sunday mornings, shared life stories and prayer requests, and went through studies together.

One of the other single moms and I clicked. Our friendship grew and our kids were practically raised together as cousins. Whenever my friend or I got sideswiped by life, we were a phone call away. We asked for advice or confirmation or admonition from each other on discipline decisions we made. We had each other to bounce ideas off of. When a mean-spirited phone call from an ex-husband, an unexpected bill, a car problem, or a health issue came up, we were each other's go-to for prayer and encouragement. We did not live together, but we did life together.

We had dinners, game nights, and movie nights. The girls had sleepovers; one of my daughters would go over to her place, while one of hers would come my way. We called it a sister swap.

At the beginning of every school year, we got together, had dinner or dessert, then shared prayer requests for the coming school year and prayed together. This was meaningful to our kids, so much so that when they went away to college, they asked to be included via speaker phone. Sharing life together during those many years took the isolation out of single parenting.

Shared Reading Time

When the kids were little, I would let them choose storybooks. As they got older, I would choose a chapter book, which everyone would enjoy. Much of the time, I read a chapter in the living room before bed or at dinner, and we talked about the story.

Reading together provided a morale booster. It was a time for sharing thoughts about the content, explaining what words meant, asking questions, expanding vocabulary, using imagination and visualization, and most of all, a love for reading.

Conclusion

I encourage parents to be intentional about the time you spend with your kids. Ask open-ended questions like "What was the best thing that happened in third grade today?" This often led them to talking about the worst part, and the stories of the day would start to unfold. Teach them to ask you and each other about their days. Kids are especially self-centered; it is our natural bent. Checking in with each other helps us be aware of others, to be attentive listeners.

Think about the legacy and the memories you want your children to have of their growing-up years. On days when you are exhausted and discouraged, it is easy to be dismissive. Some days are just going to be like that, but don't make it a pattern. When you train your ears and mind to listen, your child feels valued. Little things matter.

Your kids may not remember specific books you read or picnics you went on. They may not remember the nights they came and sat on your bed late on a school night to talk about what was on their mind, but they will remember feeling loved. They will look back on their growing-up years with warmth and fondness. They will develop character and build relationships based on what was taught and modeled at home. Make your home a place that is rich in love, laughter, and shared memories, a place where family members can let their guard down, be themselves, and belong.

Teachable Moments

I prayed God would provide me with creative disciplinary measures for my kids. I really tried to not let my kids' needs, moods, or behaviors become my anxious burden. I was learning to have grace for the bad days and things they just needed to get off their chest. Raising kids alone is challenging, and I needed God for guidance, to vent, and for insight so I could make discipline teachable moments.

Conflict Calm Down

To help everyone calm down in conflict, I had my kids put their noses on the wall for a short time. This stopped the eye contact, arguing, and fighting with another sibling or me. After a moment to calm down, we talked it through, apologized, forgave, and moved on. Acceptable apologies included, "I'm sorry for _____," so the offender took ownership, acknowledging the wrongdoing. Often all parties had to apologize, including me as Mom. It is so good for parents to apologize when they've blown it. The other party was expected to say, "I forgive you."

One of the most difficult areas for me was deciding whose fault it was in an argument or fight. Both sides gave convincing arguments and even had witnesses to back their view. However, it takes two to argue or fight. Both parties often received consequences. Sometimes I would include the parties in discussing what the consequences should be. Usually that gave them a different perspective on the

113

situation. Often, they came up with consequences more severe than I, and we discussed and compromised.

Car Rides

We've all heard it from the back seat: He touched me! Stop bothering me! She won't leave my stuff alone! While driving, I could tolerate all the loud laughing, hollering, singing, reading, and regaling of the day. Once an argument or fight broke out, I became a distracted driver. The solution I came up with was "hands on your knees." At the command "Hands on your knees," the kids had to keep their hands on their knees and be quiet until told otherwise. Sometimes *all* the kids had to do this.

Other car ride measures included pulling the car off to the side of the road until the squabbling stopped.

One time, I pulled the van over, didn't say a word, and sat there until they realized what happened. The squabbling continued, so I turned the motor off. I reminded them we would sit there until everyone was quiet. After a while, a police car pulled up and asked if there was a problem. I explained the situation to the officer, and he offered to talk to the kids. I thanked him but declined. After this, the fussing stopped, and we drove home. I never had to pull the car over that long again.

Another time, I was on the freeway and couldn't pull the van over; even with hands on knees, the arguments continued. As we neared home, I angrily yelled, "When we get home I want all of you to put—" I was going to say "put your noses on the wall," but a thought popped into my mind. (It had been a long day. We were all hot and tired. I immediately had a change of heart.) I said, "put your noses on each other's noses."

Peals of laughter filled the back seats. The mood changed in an instant when I reeled in my own feelings and had empathy toward theirs. When we pulled into the driveway, they scrambled out and stood in a circle with their noses on each other's noses, giggling. God helped me see past the immediate irritating situation and tune into my kids' hearts.

Follow-Through and Expectations

The key is to follow through and give clear expectations. Don't give any empty threats. Kids get the message that you are frustrated when you say things like, "You're grounded for life," but they also know you could not follow through with it.

Before we went into any place: the mall, the grocery store, a restaurant, the library, I explained the expected behavior and the consequences of not following those expectations. All it takes is that initial follow-through on your word, and your kids know you mean business: every time.

I remember when the kids were little, I took them to a local fast-food place with an indoor play area. They played and I got a bit of a break. Before we went in, I told them: when I call you to get your shoes, you come the first time or we will not come back. Due to past experiences, where we had left the grocery store without groceries and restaurants before eating, my kids knew I meant business.

Boundaries

As Kevin Leman states, "Guilt is a propellent for bad decisions, while hope is a propellent for good decisions." Don't let guilt manipulate you into being lenient or too harsh in your boundaries, especially in discipline and consequences. You as the adult must set and hold the limits.

Children will push to see where the boundaries are, to check their strength and stability. When those boundaries stay in place, it builds security and an understanding of expectations. If boundaries move or are inconsistent, a child or teen will continue to act out and escalate behavior. Their psyche craves knowing the parameters, so they can operate freely, confidently, and safely within those expectations.

Parents need to set boundaries for free time as well, including what goes into your kid's minds, especially preschool through elementary school. I set parameters on acceptable TV/video viewing. I would often tell my kids, "OPB or no TV" (OPB = Oregon Public Broadcasting). I knew I could trust that programming when I was making dinner or other household chores.

As my kids got to older elementary age, I taught them to guard their eyes and ears, to protect their hearts, being careful to not listen to song lyrics, TV shows, crude jokes, or inappropriate talk about someone else or themselves.

Time Management

My kids were involved in sports, band, and choir too. I set the expectations that everyone went to every concert and game, to teach them to support one another. Middle school and high school are vulnerable times; support from family while you are discovering your interests creates a buffer against a harsh world.

Children thrive in a consistent home environment. If the home is a place of upheaval and unpredictability, this can create stress that is reflected in schoolwork, behavior, and peer relationships. Work to create an environment of order and calm in your home. Set family boundaries and expectations, and guard quality family time. Work to build routines and traditions into your days and weeks, things to look forward to.

Discipline Roles and Types

In *Single Parenting That Works*, Kevin Leman says, "Homes need rules but rules are not as important as relationships. Effective discipline is a combination of words and actions. Words without actions become worthless and too much discipline just exasperates and discourages children."

Both leniency and authoritarian parenting usually result in rebellion. Your child is not your equal. This is important especially in single-parent homes. Often the only or eldest child will naturally assume that role, and it is easy for the single parent to allow this. Even though it may seem to work, this shoulders the child or teen with too many physical and emotional responsibilities.

With siblings, it will likely cause resentment and separation of relationship with that oldest sibling, if that eldest child is allowed a position of equality to the parent. There were many times that I had to remind my children they were not my equal in matters of important decisions, discipline, and so on.

Final Ideas

There is never a truer compliment or self-confidence booster than your kids overhearing you talk them up to someone else. When they hear you bragging about them to someone else, they are an accomplished baker, artist, ballplayer, and so on, or you are proud of how they included the kid who was standing alone, that really gives them a boost, so make a point of doing this every now and then.

I encourage you to be that "out" for your kids and create a secret signal so they are not left feeling pressured to do something they don't want to do. For my family, it was rubbing your nose while asking permission. If one of my kids was asked by a friend to spend the night, stay for dinner, or go somewhere they didn't want to, they rubbed their nose when asking permission. I knew my cue to say, "No, I'm sorry, you can't tonight. We have other plans," even if our plan was a normal night at home. This also worked if my kids called me on the phone to ask permission. I would ask, "Are you rubbing your nose?" They would simply have to answer yes or no.

Parenting is hard work, and we lose it at times, when we're tired, stressed, or just not paying attention. Parenting takes constant diligence and countless restarts. I have a sign in my office that says "It's Never Too Late to Start the Day Over." That is a good reminder for us and to give our children that there is always room for grace and opportunities to save face too.

In the end, strive to make decisions for your family from the basis of hope. Allow yourself to look down the road; ask yourself, Where do I see myself, my family one year, five years, ten years down the line? What character qualities do I want to instill in my child? What type of adult do I want my child to be? What reputation do I want my family, my children to have? Think and pray about these things, write down your answers, and let them guide your choices. This way, your teachable moments are centered in the big picture plans and hopes for your family.

Reflections on Childhood

I reached out to my grown children and asked them to reflect and comment on their childhood. While raising children, we as parents are forced to look at the big picture while making decisions filtered through changing circumstances. Meanwhile, our children are apt to have a completely different perspective on the same experiences. This is why I felt it was important to include their perspectives of their childhood in this book. I hope my children's insights can help parents, from all backgrounds, navigate their own journeys with a more precise compass.

Ryan

Probably the most impactful part of my childhood was the fact that we were poor. Having experience being in a lower socio-economic status helps me reframe a lot of my life in ministry and the people I have around me. Now, I do my best to make youth outings as cheap as possible. I also have lots of practice thinking outside the box on how to make things fun. There's a lot of simple things I experience now which feel like luxuries, such as buying a drink or appetizer at a restaurant and having a car (and house) with air conditioning.

We were also heavily involved with family and friends, and even though most of those relationships are pretty distant now, they make for good memories of childhood. Instead of going to places and doing stuff that would cost money, we made fun and entertainment as a group. We were encouraged to serve wherever we were, which led most of us to become deeply involved in a summer camp. So many close friendships stemmed from being involved in serving at camp.

At an age-appropriate time, [Mom] allowed us to make decisions and feel the consequences of those that were poorly made. For example, we set our own bedtime and sometimes went to school tired, or if we didn't think ahead, we'd forgot things at home. She didn't always fix it for us. Mom also taught us about finding a way, regardless of circumstances. This rubbed off so even when something seems far-fetched, I still try. When my wife and I needed a place to get married but couldn't afford a venue, I asked a venue to let us use their space in exchange for maintenance work. Even though I didn't have any connection to them, and they had someone living on-site for that purpose already [they allowed us to do it anyways].

[My mother is] resilient. Despite all the difficulties, she has held fast to her faith, continued to take care of our family, and pursued a degree, all while maintaining a confident and joyful spirit.

Cheri

Growing up through hardships was challenging, to say the least: an abusive dad, six kids, in and out of the hospital for Will, and eventually growing up in a single-parent household. I wouldn't change it for anything. I have memories and have learned so much from the life I've lived so far; maybe I'll write my own book someday.

I loved Friday night pizza night. It was such a great way to end the week: being able to spend time as a family. Our friends were always welcome, and with six kids, there were a lot of friends. Our house was the place our friends wanted to hang out, and my mom never shied away from that. Our house wasn't the cleanest, but my mom would oftentimes be the one starting games, thinking of things to do, or just letting us be loud, crazy kids with our friends.

I learned how to cook, meal plan, and make a budget from the plan she'd set up. What a great way to teach so many skills in one activity: cooking, budgeting, cooperation, problem solving, independence from an adult.

She also taught us not to take the place we live in and our days for granted. We lived in the moment and took advantage of the free/ cheap things around us. We took the Max downtown or to the zoo, we spent days by the Columbia River, or we'd take a day trip to the beach or mountain.

But what I learned the most was from my mom in the day-to-day living. It has all culminated into her teaching us to be strong, take everything one day at a time, and trust God. I can't imagine the heartache and stress my mom dealt with on a daily basis after we left our dad. As an adult, I think back to how scary it would've been to leave in the night with six kids, not knowing what the future holds.

Even with all that worry and stress, my mom never let us know about the burdens she carried, which is so important for the emotional well-being of kids. They don't know how to cope with the stress of the adults in their lives, and so often kids get burdened with their parents' burdens. Every day held new possibilities, new chances to change, new opportunities to have fun. It would have been so easy for her to give up, stay in bed, feel sorry for herself, and so on, but she never did. She worked three jobs at one point, went back to school for her bachelor's and then her master's degrees, always did her jobs/school well, and made time to have fun and care for her kids.

That strength, and her faith in Jesus, is what I admire most, and [it] pushed us towards being successful adults.

Thomas

Growing up in a single-parent home with trauma and stress affects a kid, sometimes for the better, and sometimes the worse. Each situation is different: family dynamics, personalities, learned coping mechanisms, predisposed character traits, stress levels, and so on.

My memories don't become coherent until about third grade, which was three years after we snuck out in the middle of the night to escape living with my dad.

One thing I clearly remember as a kid was my mom's unwillingness to accept the answer "No." As a kid, it was annoying, but I was expected to have things resolved when I received it as an answer from her. Hypocrisy! Double standards! Injustice! It always annoyed and frustrated me when I got denied a request.

Now as an adult, I realize that no is sometimes the best answer. Even when things seem impossible or you can't see the proverbial light, there is something better. You don't accept being in the dark or wallow in uncertainty. There's power in not knowing the outcome because you get to choose what the outcome is. If you want something out of life, and someone tells you no, you don't have to accept it just because they don't see it or can't imagine how to make it happen. Saying no, when used correctly, can be one of the most powerful words known to humankind.

My mom provided all of the essentials of living for my siblings and me. She is fun, funny, nice, caring, and loving. Some people said she was crazy because she took us camping, hiking, and on road trips, even with my brother, William, who had cerebral palsy.

I love my mom. She is so amazing because she worked every day and on Tuesdays would go to school at night. She did her homework, worked full time, and still found time for us kids. Life without her would be miserable. She makes life worth living and fun.

Reflection

As I read some of my adult kids' reflections on their growing up years, it is encouraging that their rearview mirrors are filled with day-to-day life happenings. Those experiences provide the framework for their memories, as well as their futures.

Ordinary days are such a gift, such as celebrating special days at school like science fairs, pajama days, and bingo nights. It is found in the Saturday morning bike rides and the walks to and from school. It is the simple blessings of lemonade stands, hide-and-seek, and sliding down the stairs on cardboard. I found this gift when seeing moonbeams shine over your kids as they peacefully sleep in their beds or listening to their music in the car. It is sitting around the fire pit admiring the night sky and searching for shooting stars, or late-night talks when the house is quiet and you and your teen are the only ones awake. These ordinary days of sandwiches on the go, gallons of milk in the fridge, music lessons, waiting in the parking lot at night to give a ride home from work, daily conversations, reminders, and admonitions. It is all temporary.

I am thankful that those ordinary days, a house filled with faith, love, laughter, friends, memories, and traditions are what my children carry with them as they step into adulthood. You feel your heart squeeze as you smile and say goodbye for the summer they volunteer at camp. You feel it even more when they leave to start their lives as independent adults, whether it is thousands of miles away or just ten minutes down the road. Life is theirs to face on their terms now. A new season has begun, and we continue to embrace the gift of the ordinary. Even as ordinary changes.

Wish I Had Known

As each of my kids left home and returned, I learned. I learned to show respect and give them room to grow. I learned to allow myself to grow as our relationships changed. It was hard transitioning out of the role and responsibilities of being a full-time Mom. I prayed God would give me wisdom and creativity to approach situations in a new way.

Here are a few things I wish I had known about my adult kids.

When my adult kids first moved back home, it felt like things were falling back into place. Yet, that rosy picture did not last long. It was difficult for my adult children to move back after being independent individuals out in the world. Siblings struggled with intolerance, slipping into old behaviors while also wanting to be independent.

I wish I had known to have a shared discussion about their desires and expectations, as well as mine, before a joyous homecoming. I wish I had drawn up written expectations of household maintenance, responsibilities, and timelines for accomplishing tasks. I wish I had a discussion about bathroom use, daily schedules, and meal planning. I wish we had covered the question: how will you contribute financially or otherwise to the home?

When my college kids came home for the summer, they had had a school year of independence. At college, they did not have to tell anyone where they were going or when they would be back. They did not have to explain to anyone why they skipped class, called in sick to work, or stayed up all night to write a paper. They had embraced autonomy.

I wish I would have known to approach new situations with a sense of humor and grace. One of my sons sold his car when he left college. He felt uncomfortable asking to use a car or to ask for rides when he came home. Another kid, home from college, started putting their name on food, in the house they had purchased. I expressed that we are a family; everything in the kitchen is for you to help yourself, like we've always done it. Ah, those famous words: "like we've always done it."

At one time, my son and his wife moved in with me while their house was being built. They agreed to help renovate my home while living with me and working full-time jobs. I found it is different having a married couple live with you. I knew I had to give them space and time to be their own unit. They were super busy with their work, building their house, ministry, and so on, and I did not expect them to carve out consistent time with me. I realized their room was their home, and after a long day, they wanted to retire to their own space.

Reflection

It's important to give our adult children the latitude to establish their new relationship with us as their parents. We want our kids to feel comfortable around us, to open up to us. If they feel we have our thumb on them, they will shut down and avoid us. Your job of raising a child is done when they reach adulthood. Then is the time to establish open communication and mutual respect. Remember, "Let your conversation be always full of grace, seasoned with salt, so that you may know how to answer everyone" (Colossians 4:6).

I am truly an empty-nester now. I am proud to see my kids' accomplishments and watch them build their lives. My son and his wife are living in the home they helped build, about ten minutes down the road from me. A few years ago, two of my kids took jobs in different states. While I do in some ways miss the shared living space and seeing my kids more regularly; I am content. I am developing my own routine and enjoy the visits from my kids when they stop by, planned and unexpectedly.

For those of you with teenagers or kids in college, I suggest to hold your kids with open hands. Begin to change the conversations from "You should," "You ought," and "Why didn't you …?" to "What are your thoughts? How can I help? What do you think the next steps should be? Bummer that *that* happened, what do you think you'll do about it?"

Adult kids naturally pull away as they establish themselves. They may pull away from the faith and the lifestyle in which they were raised. They may even see you, the parent who has loved them, stood up for them, and cared for them, as the enemy. They may blame you, judge you, and list your shortcomings. Hold fast. You cannot stand toe to toe with your adult child arguing your point without losing some ground. Instead, take it to the Lord, and remember, "Therefore confess your sins to each other and pray for each other so that you may be healed. The prayer of a righteous person is powerful and effective" (James 5:16b).

Whatever happens in your adult child's life, based on their choices or life's circumstances, is between them and God now. These are things I've learned and advise. These are not things that I always did right but Remember, you are now a benchwarmer, watching and praying until you are called in to help or advise. God is writing their story. We are to stand with our huge foam finger, cheering, "You got this. I'm in your corner. Hang in there." It is hard to be on the sidelines and watch our kids face pain and endure hard consequences. But remember, we had to face life's hard knocks too, and we learned from each of them. Now we let our adult kids grow closer to God, in similar ways: through experiences of strengthening and understanding. While our children may not see our boundless love, they know in their hearts, we are on their side fighting for them: on our knees.

PLAN A

Conclusion

You've just navigated some very challenging, yet rewarding terrain; walking alongside me through the vulnerable expressions of an abused wife and single mom. It is my hope that you've connected with some "I've been there" snapshots along the trail.

I once had the idea, maybe from an incorrect teaching, that God has Plan A for your life, and that is the primo plan. It likely stems from Jeremiah 29:11: "For I know the plans I have for you." I believed that before you are even born, God has specific expectations, a job, calling, place, and purpose for you to fulfill and accomplish.

As a teen and in my early twenties, I just knew I blew it. My mind and heart were bound to God, but in different settings; it was like I lost all willpower. It felt as Paul writes in Romans 7:15, "I do not understand what I do. For what I want to do I do not do but what I hate, I do." I was outwardly living for God but secretly attempting to find my worth in inappropriate relationships. This ironically led to a decline in my sense of worth and self-esteem.

That specific, predetermined Plan A for my life, I just knew I messed it up completely. I believed God was disappointed in me, and I hated myself for it. I believed I couldn't be or do what He had intended. I assumed God was like a coach who turns aside when we mess up the play and focuses His attention on star players. I determined He would choose someone else for Plan A, and because of my poor choices, I would have to settle for Plan B.

I took my Plan B seriously as a proud wife and mother. I worked with all my heart to honor the Lord with this responsibility and role. Yet in the back of my mind, I would sometimes wonder, what was that Plan A I had ruined?

Through my journey, I hope you see I never ruined a Plan A. God does not look upon me, or you, with disappointment. When we make mistakes, it doesn't cause God to back away or quit speaking. He doesn't count us out or give our life's plan to someone else when we mess up.

As you see through these stories, God has and continues to walk with me down life's path; showing me immense grace and forgiveness. He hurts when I hurt; He understands my pain better than I do. God knows exactly who I am, my strengths and weaknesses. He will use especially the weaknesses and mistakes of my past to honor Him. As Romans 8:28 shares, "We know that in all things God works for the good of those who love him, who have been called according to his purpose." I encourage you to trust that God will do the same for your journey as well.

As you know, I did not experience this journey alone; as adults, my kids have taken their pain and scars, and used them to stand for justice. They try to speak and act for those less fortunate, to mentor and positively influence others in their lives. I pray the same will be true for the painful experiences you and your loved ones have endured.

I hope you have found in my stories that God loves to walk with us through life's beautiful meadows, challenging climbs, and treacherous mountains. God trudges through life's deep muck with us, tenderly guiding, comforting, and encouraging us on the trails. Like those red galoshes from my childhood, God covers us and protects us in the difficult moments of our everyday lives.

Each in our own ways, my children and I have learned to don those red galoshes and show others how to put them on too so the muck and messes of life become impenetrable to the soul.

My hope is that my journey is a guidebook for you. I encourage you to put on your red galoshes as you go through puddles and debris in your daily path. You are now prepared to watch the dirty water and sludge of life circumstances splash up against you and slide right off. With God's presence, we know circumstances cannot dampen our shoes, socks, or spirits.

BIBLIOGRAPHY

Abuse Recovery Ministry Services,
https://abuserecovery.org.

"The Life of a Single Mom,"
https://thelifeofasinglemom.com.

Brad Harper and Drew Harper,
Space at the Table (2016),

Caleb Kaltenbach, *Messy Grace: How a Pastor with Gay Parents Learned to Love Others without Sacrificing Conviction* (2015).

Jackie Hill Perry, *Gay Girl, Good God* (2018).

Ed Shaw, *Same Sex Attraction and the Church* (2015).

A message from my brother:

I am glad that Ann is able to share her story with us. Many of her close family and friends see her love and compassion for them first. She does not come across as a victim, instead she is the one reaching out to encourage and help others, sometimes disregarding her own struggles.

People, including me, see her as courageous, unafraid to take on any challenge for a proper cause. They see her as unstoppable, willing to continue through thick and thin until the goal is met. Add to this a big heart. She has the ability in the midst of a struggle to notice others hurting around her and to be able to step in with compassion, wisdom and encouragement to lift them up and get them going while she is pushing herself along.

In this book we get to look deeper into a complex woman with a big heart. She was not gifted with great opportunities or lucky chances. Her strength is her faith that God was in control, which kept her going. Her gift to us reading this book is the encouragement that even in our own circumstances we can come out on top. We can keep going keep believing and keep reaching out to others along the way.

In Ann's Wake of life she leaves family, friends, students and even acquaintances that have been changed by her heart and tenacity. You will glean from the wisdom that she has gained along the way. You will feel the keen sense of humor and great compassion and love that will reach out to you from these pages. A brush with Ann will put a tear in your eye, great laughter, and a very warm heart.

Reader, you are about to endeavor on an adventure. If Ann could have seen all that was going to happen before it happened, she may have given up early. Instead, she has made it through to today. She has given this story that we have in our hand that will touch us, encourage us, strengthen our faith and change us for having read it.

A message from my sister:

Nothing broke her stride! Not even an abusive husband slowed her down. She kept moving along even as a single mom of 6. Her voice is strength and her strength is her faith in God!